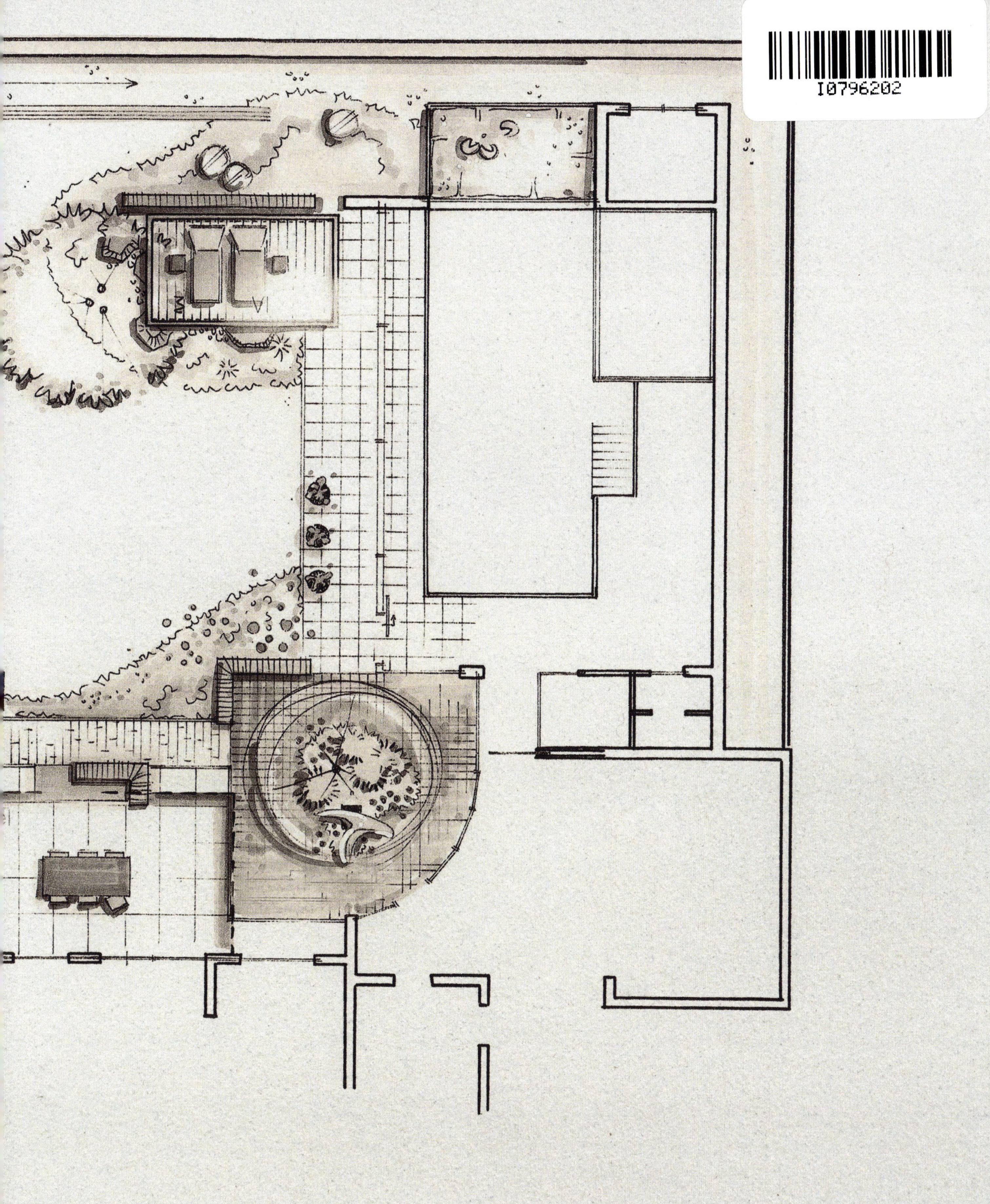

JAPANDI OUTDOOR LIVING

LAILA RIETBERGEN

Lannoo

Contents

Preface

I would like to start by thanking you for having my third Japandi book (I really have to pinch myself writing this) in front of you and for your interest in reading and learning about this wonderful aesthetic. In both of my first two books, *Japandi Living – Japanese tradition. Scandinavian design.* and *Japandi – Serene homes & Thoughtful living*, the focus is on interiors. In this book, I would love to delve into the world of Japandi outdoor living.

When I started writing my first book in 2021, Japandi wasn't as well known as it is now in 2025 – today you see it popping up everywhere. For me, Japandi isn't a trend of natural colours and organic shapes. It's inseparably linked to Japanese and Scandinavian philosophies, to craftsmanship, items that last, natural materials, showing ageing and working with – instead of against – nature. These are all more important to me than the colours you use. Just like in my previous two books, here, too I will share my take on Japandi and highlight some of its most important elements to me.

It probably comes as no surprise that nature and natural materials are essential in Japandi. In Japanese and Scandinavian cultures, spending time outside is important. Of course, going forest bathing (*shinrin-yoku*) or getting a breath of fresh air on the beach is lovely. But what about your own piece of nature, your own garden, courtyard or (small) balcony? This is the space you see and can enjoy every day. In this book, I'd like to invite you to explore different Japandi outdoor spaces so you can learn about what's important and collect lots of practical tips regardless of the size of your outdoor space.

Maybe you've been lovingly integrating Japandi for many years, or perhaps this is your first encounter with this design aesthetic. Either way, I hope my book and thoughts inspire you and help you make your home and outside space into somewhere you can recharge, have fun and connect with everyone in it.

Love, Laila

About the author

'I have never tried that before, so I think I can definitely do it.'
Pippi Långstrump (created by the Swedish author Astrid Lindgren)

I really like this quote as I think it perfectly sums up my journey and personality. I studied sports marketing at the Johan Cruyff Institute in the Netherlands – and I still love sports – but I was also one of those girls who was always changing her bedroom. I inherited this love for interiors from my mother and when I decided it was time to start my own business, I really wanted it to revolve around interior design.

In October 2020 I started my account, @japandi.interior, on Instagram – a perfect way for me to inspire people around the globe with my take on the Japandi philosophy. In 2021 I started writing my first book and I'm so happy to share that over 12,000 copies of that book have been sold already. Partly thanks to my books, I discovered that I like to create (tangible) products as well. So in 2024 I launched a lime paint collection with over 35 colours in collaboration with Betonlook – and I'm working on some new products already. I'm so glad that I have found my *ikigai* and am looking forward to all those 'Pippi moments' that the future holds.

My personal interior style wasn't always as Japandi as it is today, but – being the chaotic person I am – I've always been drawn to a more tranquil home environment to bring me the calm and serenity my busy brain needs. I've also always loved bringing the outside in, with natural materials and (lots of) plants. Together with my boyfriend Wouter, son Tygo and cat Kiyomi, I live in the Netherlands. Here, we have created our own version of Japandi in our new home and I'm happy to say it meets all of our needs. We're looking forward to growing together and of course changing things in the house to keep it fun and safe for Tygo.

I hope my book and thoughts inspire you to find your take on Japandi and maybe even dare to create your own Pippi moments.

About this book

In this book, I invite you to explore the art of outdoor minimalism and discover how to create your own outdoor sanctuary – one that feels like a natural extension of your indoor space. For me it's not about following strict rules, but about embracing the feeling it brings: calm, connection and simplicity.

If you've read one of my previous books on Japandi interior design or follow me on Instagram, you probably already know that, to me, Japandi is more than just a design style. It's a way of living or mindset. A quiet return to the essence of things. Deeply connected to nature in many ways, Japandi is rooted in simplicity. It invites us to live with intention, to find beauty in the understated, to accept perfect imperfections and to create spaces that breathe.

Japandi is a fusion of two worlds: the refined minimalism and traditions of Japan combined with the soft, functional warmth of Scandinavian design. Together, they form spaces that are serene, grounded and purposeful, offering not just visual harmony, but also emotional clarity. Personally, I see it as the perfect marriage. It's a blend that allows you to make it your own, drawing from the best of both cultures. I believe it's essential to shape your living space – indoors and out – in a way that truly reflects who you are. Not by copying everything you see, but by choosing what you genuinely love, even if it doesn't fit perfectly within the traditional boundaries of Japandi. And maybe that's the beauty of it.

At its core, Japandi is about balance: between light and shadow, form and function, tradition and innovation. It's not loud. It doesn't try to impress. Instead, it invites us to slow down and notice – the grain of the wood, the space between stones, the play of sunlight through leaves and branches.

The principles and philosophies of Japandi translate beautifully to both indoor and outdoor spaces. In this book, I'll explore the Japandi lifestyle as a whole, showing how it can shape your outdoor environment and how to create a smooth, natural flow between inside and outside.

As I emphasise in all my books about the aesthetic, these are my ideas of how to live this (life)style. The great thing is, you're free to make it your own, as much or as little as you want. Just choose the parts that work for you. And I hope you enjoy this book as much as I enjoyed creating it.

CHAPTER ONE

In harmony with nature

In this chapter, we explore how the gentle interplay of simplicity, balance and natural beauty can transform outdoor spaces into living works of art. No matter the size of the space, the Japandi approach helps create a place where you can relax, recharge, feel at ease, and entertain with intention.

Inspired by the timeless traditions of Japan and the clean, sustainable ethos of Scandinavia, Japandi design celebrates harmony, functionality, warmth and minimalist elegance. By bringing this philosophy to your outdoor areas, you can create a seamless flow between indoors and out, blurring the boundaries and inviting nature in.

At the heart of Japandi lies a deep respect for nature and natural materials. Wood, stone, bamboo and linen are chosen not just for their durability and tactile beauty, but also for how they evolve gracefully over time. Their organic textures and muted hues remind us of the raw beauty of the natural world, reinforcing Japandi's commitment to authenticity and sustainability.

This design philosophy turns outdoor spaces into ever-changing canvases, where the interplay of light, shadow and seasonal shifts becomes an integral part of the experience. Even indoors, shadows – like those cast by swaying tree branches just outside your window – can echo the outside world, connecting the two realms. By embracing the imperfections of nature, Japandi creates environments that feel grounded, timeless and tranquil. It encourages us to slow down and appreciate the quiet dialogue between human craftsmanship and the wild, imperfect beauty of the earth.

Japandi outdoor living is about embracing imperfections – not just accepting them, but also highlighting them. Like *kintsugi*, the Japanese art of repairing broken pottery with gold, where the cracks aren't hidden but illuminated. The flaws become part of the story, part of the beauty. They remind us that brokenness isn't the end, but that it can be a new beginning, made stronger and more meaningful than before.

Core principles of Japandi

Japandi is more than just a collection of colours on a wall or a passing interior trend – it's not 'just a style'. It's a mindset, a way of living that goes far deeper than surface aesthetics. At its core, Japandi blends the thoughtful calm of Japanese tradition with the functional warmth of Scandinavian design. The result is a holistic philosophy that can be felt in every detail, especially when applied to the spaces we live in, both indoors and out.

Unsurprisingly, the core principles of Japandi are closely tied to the philosophies that shape both cultures. In Japan and Scandinavia alike, design is not only about how something looks, but also about how it makes you feel: how it supports your life, enhances your connection with nature and fosters well-being.

Before we explore these philosophies in depth, I'd love to take a moment to briefly outline the key principles that form the foundation of Japandi design – principles that guide not just the way we decorate a space, but also how we experience and live in it.

Minimalism and decluttering

As boring as it may sound, I truly believe that every home and style looks and feels better when it's decluttered. In Japandi design, however, decluttering isn't just a nice-to-have – it's essential. While we often associate decluttering with interiors, your outdoor space deserves the same attention. Take a look at your garden, balcony or terrace: do you really need to place the garbage in sight or leave garden tools out in several places in your garden? A tidy, intentional outdoor space instantly feels more peaceful and refined.

Personally, I really like the 80/20 principle: keep 80% of your belongings out of sight and let just 20% remain visible. You can use this rule for your outside space, too. Of course, it depends on how much you own and it's a bit different outdoors than indoors, but it's a great rule of thumb. Look around, declutter, donate, sell, and create storage for the things you genuinely need or love. Grouping similar items together can also reduce visual clutter.

Think about clever solutions like built-in benches with hidden storage, clean-lined shelving for beautiful essentials, or tucking away tools in a neat cabinet. When you strip away the excess, every remaining piece – whether it's furniture, a plant pot or sculptural feature – gains presence and meaning. In this way, minimalism brings calm, clarity and a touch of elegance to your outdoor space.

'Minimalism encourages intentional living. When planning a garden, I believe in not exceeding sizes or amounts that don't serve any purpose.'

Annika Zetterman – garden designer

Balance and harmony

In a Japandi garden, balance and harmony are not about symmetry, but about creating a dialogue between elements. Think of the contrast between rough stone and soft moss, the stillness of gravel beside bamboo blowing in the breeze, or the quiet rhythm of stepping stones that guide you through the space. These relationships are intentional but never forced.

In Japanese philosophy, harmony (*wa*) is seen as a fundamental value. It encourages cooperation, coexistence and gentle respect between different forces – nature and human, stillness and motion, full and empty. In Scandinavian thought, this same concept appears in the way natural materials, muted tones and simple lines work together without noise or competition.

When these values meet in a Japandi garden, the result is a space that feels grounded and alive: not overwhelming or empty, but gently in tune. Every element, from a bench to a single potted plant, has a role to play and space to breathe.

There are multiple ways to create balance and harmony in your garden or on your patio or balcony. Use contrasting textures and shapes by pairing, for example, rough stone with soft foliage, or sleek furniture with organic ceramics. Let these opposites highlight each other. Also, in line with the previous principle, avoid crowding and allow for moments of *Ma* (see page 38) – intentional emptiness. A single tree in a bed of gravel can say more than 10 mismatched shrubs.

Harmony is not just about objects and how they relate to each other. Harmony also arises when an outdoor space is in tune with the place it is located. That's why you should consider the type of greenery you plant in your garden, so that your little piece of the natural world lives in harmony with the flora and fauna that inhabit your surroundings.

Materials, textures and shapes

From the warmth of hand-carved wood to the calming coolness of stone, Japandi design is rooted in the honest beauty of materials that grow richer with time. These natural, tactile elements not only bring a grounded serenity to a space, but also carry a quiet narrative of authenticity, tradition and a respectful connection to nature. They remind us that nothing in the natural world is rushed or over-polished; it simply evolves, gracefully and with purpose.

Texture plays a key role, too. The contrast between rough stone and soft linen, or between smooth ceramic and raw concrete, creates subtle layers that feel calm, not cluttered. It's an amazing way to create contrast without being loud. The same goes for shapes. If you have lots of straight lines in your garden, like fencing and terrace stones, you can break up those lines, for example, by choosing a dining table and chairs with more round and/or organic shapes.

Whether you're designing a small city balcony, a courtyard filled with dappled light or a wide, open garden, the Japandi approach encourages you to work with materials that breathe, age and carry the soul of the natural world. In doing so, outdoor living becomes more than just a style. It becomes a quiet ritual of connection, balance and enduring beauty.

Functionality – beauty with purpose

In Japandi, functionality isn't hidden, but celebrated. It's what gives a space honesty and longevity. This principle becomes especially powerful in the garden, where nature and design are meant to coexist, not compete. A functional Japandi outdoor space is not about filling every corner, but about making each element earn its place. A bench isn't just seating; it offers rest, reflects simplicity and invites presence. A stone path doesn't just connect spaces; it slows movement, encourages mindfulness and leads the eye with intention.

Functionality also means flexibility. Multi-purpose design allows outdoor areas – whether balconies, courtyards or larger gardens – to remain uncluttered while still being deeply usable. For example, a bench with space to store cushions or a side table that can be used as a stool when you have more people over.

By embracing functionality, your Japandi garden becomes more than simply a beautiful setting. It becomes a space that supports your daily rhythm, encourages presence and honours simplicity, allowing life and landscape to move in quiet harmony.

Sustainability – quiet choices, lasting impact

Sustainability isn't a mere trend in the aesthetic, but a mindset. It's the quiet belief that what we bring into our homes and gardens should last, serve a purpose and exist in respectful dialogue with the natural world. In outdoor spaces, this principle becomes especially visible and essential.

Sustainability in Japandi isn't just about recycled materials or eco-certifications (though those matter, too). It's about choosing fewer and better things. It's about investing in items that age gracefully, repair easily and don't need replacing with every passing season. A solid teak bench, a handcrafted ceramic pot, a well-made linen cushion – these pieces aren't disposable. They're chosen for their quality, their story, and their ability to endure both time and weather.

This principle extends into how we treat our spaces. Rather than over-designing or filling a garden with fast-growing, short-lived plants or synthetic materials, Japandi encourages restraint. It asks what you really need and what will last. Simplicity becomes sustainable when it's intentional – when every choice is made with awareness of its impact, not just on the environment, but also on your sense of peace and presence.

Sustainability also means working *with* nature, not against it. Like collecting rainwater for irrigation. Choose native plants and low-maintenance species that thrive in your climate. I will share loads more about plant choice later on (see page 213). Allow certain materials, like untreated wood or oxidised stone, to weather naturally. Design with the seasons in mind, embracing rather than fighting change.

By weaving sustainability into your outdoor space, you're not just creating a garden, but cultivating a philosophy. One that values craftsmanship over consumption, presence over perfection, and beauty that doesn't fade, but deepens.

Choosing solar lighting or LED fixtures with timers is a great way to save energy.

The philosophies of the Japandi garden

Before a single stone is placed or a path is drawn, a Japandi garden begins with a thought – a philosophy. They are the quiet roots beneath every Japandi garden. These outdoor spaces are not just designed for beauty or function; they are grounded in deeper ideas about how we live, what we value and how we relate to the natural world.

From the Zen-inspired calm of Japanese traditions to the soulful simplicity of Nordic living, Japandi gardens are born from a blend of cultural wisdoms that share one powerful belief: that nature is not separate from us, but a part of us.

In this section, we explore the philosophies that breathe life into Japandi design. Principles that go beyond trends or aesthetics. These ideas shape everything: the placement of a single rock, the texture of a bench, the choice to leave a space empty. They invite us to design not just with the eye, but also with the heart. As you read, let these timeless concepts guide your creative process. They are the invisible threads that turn a garden into a sanctuary.

Japanese garden philosophies

There are many intriguing Japanese philosophies, and I love sharing several of them. I'll briefly introduce a few and then we'll explore a selection more deeply.

Wabi-sabi - the beauty of imperfection

You may have heard of the philosophy *wabi-sabi*, or even read about it in one of my previous books, which celebrates the beauty of imperfection. This philosophy teaches us to appreciate the natural ebb and flow of life, acknowledging that true beauty often lies in asymmetry and the quiet interplay between light and shadow. Rather than hiding flaws, wabi-sabi honours them. A garden stone cracked by time, a wooden bench weathered by seasons or a leaf slowly turning colour – each is a reflection of life's natural cycles. Wabi-sabi asks us to pause, observe and embrace the imperfect and impermanent.

In Japandi design, this translates to spaces that are soulful, organic and rich with quiet beauty. Use weathered wood benches or stone lanterns with moss. Embrace patina and natural ageing in your materials.

Kanso - calmness and the quiet power of understatement

Kanso is the Japanese principle that celebrates simplicity – not as an aesthetic trend, but as a mindful practice. Rooted in Zen Buddhism, it invites us to eliminate clutter and distractions, allowing only what is essential and meaningful to remain. This isn't about being minimal for minimalism's sake, but about creating spaces with purpose and intention. In kanso, every object and element should serve a clear role, whether practical or emotional. It values clarity, calmness and the quiet power of understatement, making space for the spirit to breathe.

In a Japandi outdoor setting, kanso can be expressed by designing with restraint: using fewer materials, neutral colour palettes and clean lines. Whether it's a single sculptural boulder in a raked gravel bed or a small, well-placed wooden bench, the focus is on simplicity that feels peaceful, not empty.

'I choose natural materials that weather beautifully: stone softened by moss, wood that gracefully silvers. I don't design for perfection on day one, but for a deeper beauty that reveals itself over the years.'

Noël van Mierlo – garden designer

Mottainai - a kind reminder for sustainable living

Mottainai is more than just a word – it's an ethos. Often translated as 'what a waste', it expresses regret over waste and a deep respect for resources. It calls for reusing, repairing and cherishing what we have. This philosophy is deeply sustainable.

Historically, mottainai was embedded in everyday life. Scraps of fabric were mended and reused, broken ceramics were repaired with care, and food was never wasted without reflection. In gardens, too, this principle was present. Fallen leaves were allowed to decompose and nourish the soil, rainwater was captured for reuse, and aged stones or wood were treasured for the stories they carried.

In a modern Japandi garden, mottainai might show up in subtle but powerful ways. Repurposing old materials – weathered bricks, salvaged wood, rusted metal – adds texture and soul. Choosing native or climate-adapted plants reduces waste and honours the local environment. Composting, collecting rainwater, or designing for low maintenance are all quiet affirmations of mottainai.

Gaman - bend without breaking

Gaman is about patience, endurance and quiet strength. It's the stoic perseverance to stay grounded despite hardship. In garden design, it can be reflected in resilient plants, long-lasting materials or thoughtful seasonal planning. It reminds us that beauty often takes time to unfold. Gaman builds character into space.

Gaman also complements the Scandinavian concept of simplicity – living well with less, enduring long winters with patience and humility, and finding contentment in modest beauty.

Together, these traditions cultivate not just aesthetic harmony, but also emotional resilience. A Japandi garden, then, becomes more than a place of beauty – it becomes a space for practicing gaman: the strength to be still, to wait, to endure gently, and to bloom again when the time is right.

Ma – the power of the in-between

In much of Western design, emphasis is placed on the tangible: the objects, the plants, the structures that occupy space. But in Japanese aesthetics, and by extension in Japandi design, there is equal – if not greater – value placed on the space between those objects. This concept is known as *Ma*. Ma is the pause, the interval, the silence that exists between things. It is the emptiness that allows presence to be felt. It is not merely a void, but a meaningful absence, a moment of stillness that gives context and depth to everything around it.

Historically, Ma originates from ancient Japanese philosophy, rooted in Shinto and Zen Buddhist thought, where space and time are viewed as interconnected. In traditional Japanese architecture, such as in tea houses or temples, Ma is expressed through sliding doors (*shoji*), open verandas, and quiet in-between spaces that encourage reflection. The idea is that beauty lies not only in form, but also in the breathing space between forms, where nature and human presence coexist in harmony.

At its essence, Ma is the invisible thread that ties a space together. It's the blank wall that gives artwork its voice, the pause in music that creates rhythm, the open courtyard that lends weight to the structures surrounding it. In nature, Ma appears as the clearing that lets light filter through the trees, or the space between a stepping stone and a moss bed that invites deliberate movement and mindfulness.

In everyday life, embracing Ma means welcoming pauses and breathing space – whether that's leaving gaps in your schedule for rest, simplifying your possessions or allowing conversations room for silence. It's a mindset of intentional pacing and presence, rather than constant filling and doing. In Japandi garden design, Ma becomes a powerful tool to cultivate calm, clarity and visual harmony.

Rather than filling every space with plants or furniture, you allow for intentional emptiness: a gravel bed between pavers, a quiet zone of untouched soil, or the deliberate space between a bench and a sculptural tree. These spaces allow light, shadow and the rhythm of nature to emerge, giving your garden a sense of peace and balance. As you'll read in the section on layout (see page 118), implementing Ma isn't about subtracting life – it's about allowing life to flow more naturally. With Ma, the garden doesn't speak more loudly, but more deeply.

'I often use lawn, unmown grass, subtle gravel or stone surfaces, ground covers or water to create pauses between more richly planted areas. These quiet zones allow other elements to stand out.'

Noël van Mierlo – garden designer

Shizen – the natural way

Shizen translates to 'naturalness' or 'nature's way' in Japanese. It is a core aesthetic and philosophical principle in Japanese culture that values the unforced, the spontaneous and the authentic. Rooted in Taoist and Shinto beliefs, shizen reflects a reverence for nature not as something to dominate, but as something to harmonise with. It celebrates the inherent beauty of the world when left to evolve organically, with all its irregularities and imperfections.

In design, shizen encourages the use of natural materials, gentle transitions and irregular forms that evoke the quiet rhythms of nature. In a Japandi-style garden, shizen comes to life in seamless transitions between the built environment and the wild. A stone path might disappear into a patch of moss. Decking may blur into the garden with no harsh border. Plants are chosen not for their perfection, but for their texture, movement and ability to age gracefully. Even the arrangement of objects follows a natural rhythm, not strict symmetry.

Japanese gardens embracing shizen do not aim to tame nature into strict order; rather, they seek to reveal its quiet, underlying harmony. Trees are pruned to highlight their most graceful branches, not to conform to a shape. Rocks are arranged asymmetrically to suggest movement or stillness. Water, or its abstracted presence in raked gravel, flows softly to guide the eye and calm the spirit. This dialogue with nature creates a sense of peace and authenticity that is timeless.

Ultimately, shizen is not just a design approach; it's a world view. It invites us to step back, listen to the rhythm of the natural world, and design spaces that respect and reflect that gentle order.

You can implement shizen in your garden by:

- Using natural, untreated materials like wood, stone and clay.
- Allowing native or adaptive plants to grow with minimal intervention.
- Choosing irregular forms and asymmetry in layout and placement.
- Creating soft transitions between different zones – no hard edges.
- Leaving room for natural ageing and weathering; patina is welcomed.

The philosophy of shakkei – borrowed scenery as a living canvas

One of the most poetic and transformative principles in traditional Japanese garden design is *shakkei*, which translates to 'borrowed scenery'. At its essence, shakkei is the art of thoughtfully framing and incorporating the natural surroundings – mountains, forests, neighbouring rooftops or even the sky – into the design of the garden. The result is a seamless, harmonious dialogue between the curated and the wild, the near and the distant.

This principle allows the garden to appear larger and more immersive than it actually is. A well-placed window, an opening between trees or a strategically lowered fence can turn a distant hill or grove of bamboo into part of your garden's visual composition. In this way, nature becomes your co-designer, and the garden no longer ends at the boundary, but continues to breathe beyond it.

The philosophy of shakkei dates back to ancient Chinese landscape painting and garden design, and was embraced and refined in Japan during the Heian (794–1185) and Edo (1603–1868) periods. Aristocratic villas and Zen temples alike were carefully positioned to maximise views of surrounding nature. The technique was especially prized in Karesansui (Zen) and Tsukiyama (hill) gardens, where the sight of distant mountains or forest edges would complete the sense of depth and stillness. I share more about these gardens on pages 65 and 68.

Shakkei isn't just about what you see; it's also about feeling connected to a larger whole. It invites humility by reminding us that no design exists in isolation. Nature is not to be controlled, but to be respectfully observed, framed and honoured.

Allowing nature to take its course can be done in subtle ways. Leave a corner of your garden a little wilder. Leave seed heads untouched in winter for birds to feed on, or allow fallen leaves to rest in a corner where insects can shelter. A small log pile tucked away creates a home for beetles. These quiet choices let nature breathe in your garden—beautiful, practical, and full of life.

Scandinavian garden philosophies

There are many fascinating Scandinavian philosophies. It is no surprise that there are many books written about them. Reading about these philosophies also shows us the link between Japan and Scandinavia. I will share several of them and connect them to the garden.

Hygge and koselig - that special feeling

Hygge is the Danish art of comfort, connection and contentment. It is often associated with cosy blankets and candlelight, but its spirit runs deeper. Hygge means creating an atmosphere where people feel safe, calm and connected. In outdoor design, hygge reveals itself in inviting seating areas, natural materials that age gracefully, and thoughtful lighting that glows softly in the evening. It's the feeling of sitting under a tree with a warm drink, surrounded by the gentle quiet of a well-loved garden.

Koselig is the Norwegian counterpart to the Danish hygge, emphasizing warmth, comfort and a sense of belonging. It involves creating inviting environments that foster intimacy and happiness. This philosophy values simple pleasures and togetherness. In design, it encourages warm textures and welcoming spaces.

Sisu - Inner strength

Sisu is the Finnish concept of determination, resilience and courage in the face of adversity. It reflects an inner strength and the ability to sustain action against the odds. This philosophy encourages pushing beyond perceived limits. The kind of strength that's not loud, but deeply rooted. In design, it can inspire durable and enduring elements. In a garden, it means incorporating hardy, low-maintenance plants and materials that withstand various weather conditions, symbolising resilience and lasting beauty.

Mutability - embracing change

Mutability acknowledges the constant change in nature and life, encouraging adaptability and resilience. It promotes flexibility and openness to transformation, supporting dynamic and evolving environments. In design, it leads to spaces that can adapt to different needs and seasons. In a garden, it means incorporating elements that change with the seasons, such as deciduous plants or movable furniture, allowing the garden to evolve and adapt over time.

Friluftsliv - connection with nature

Freely translated, *friluftsliv* means 'free air life' or 'open-air living' and is deeply rooted in the Norwegian (and broadly Scandinavian) philosophy that celebrates the simple, daily connection with nature – regardless of weather, wealth or season. It's not about outdoor activities in the sporty sense, but about being present and grounded in natural surroundings for emotional well-being, balance and resilience. It embodies a way of life rather than a hobby: being outdoors is not a luxury; it's a necessity for the soul. To infuse the spirit of friluftsliv into your Japandi garden, aim to create outdoor spaces that invite everyday use, deep sensory connection and slow, restorative interaction with the natural world.

Friluftsliv isn't a seasonal, but a year-round engagement, so one way to implement it into your outdoor space is to design it with all seasons in mind. Think about including sheltered areas with canopies, pergolas or even tree cover for shade or rain protection. Add fire elements: a fire bowl, wood stove or even candlelight to extend use into colder seasons. And use evergreen plants, grasses or moss to maintain a sense of life through winter. Also consider movable furniture to adapt to weather or sunlight.

Lys – the embrace of light

In the Scandinavian world – especially in Denmark and Norway – light is not merely a functional necessity, but a cherished companion. With long, dark winters and fleeting summer days, *lys* (pronounced lees, meaning 'light') carries deep emotional and cultural significance. It's more than illumination; it's warmth, clarity, hope and a sense of quiet joy woven into everyday life.

Lys is the soft glow of morning sunlight spilling across pale wooden floors. It's the golden hue of a summer evening sky and the comforting flicker of a candlelit corner during the stillness of winter. In Nordic living, light is embraced and honoured as a life-giving force that elevates both spirit and space. It isn't about brightness for its own sake, but about gentle illumination that soothes rather than overwhelms – a subtle presence that invites calm and introspection.

In Japandi design, where Japanese mindfulness meets Scandinavian warmth, lys becomes more than a physical quality – it becomes a silent storyteller. Both Japanese and Scandinavian aesthetics deeply understand the interplay between light and shadow. In gardens, this might appear as filtered sunlight cascading through bamboo screens, the soft flicker of a lantern at dusk, or the way bare winter branches cast intricate patterns on the earth below. Light is not just a design feature; it's also a living presence. A quiet rhythm. A mood. A connection between your home, your garden and the changing sky above.

Designing with lys in mind means being intentional about how light interacts with your outdoor space. It means placing a bench where the morning sun gently lands, using natural materials that absorb and reflect light softly, and allowing shadows to dance gracefully across stone, wood and foliage. Every hour and each season offers a slightly different expression of light, bringing movement and mood to a still landscape.

From the golden twilight of Nordic summers to the hushed dimness of snow-covered evenings, lys connects people to the rhythms of nature. It evokes serenity and presence, reminding us to slow down, look up and feel the moment.

'The light is very special in the Nordics, affecting the people and everything else that lives there. Every year, we experience the full circle of life, from the vivid summer light when the sun never sets to the compact darkness of winter.'

Annika Zetterman – garden designer

Lagom – the art of 'just enough'

Lagom is a typical Swedish concept with no direct translation in English, yet its meaning resonates universally: not too much, not too little – just enough. Rooted in centuries of Scandinavian cultural and environmental wisdom, lagom reflects a lifestyle of balance, sustainability and quiet contentment. It is neither indulgent nor austere, but rather a mindful middle path that values harmony in all aspects of life.

Historically, lagom arose from the Swedish agrarian tradition, where communities survived by taking only what was needed, sharing resources fairly and living within their means. This collective sense of moderation and fairness shaped not just social values, but also the Scandinavian approach to design and daily life. In modern times, it has become a philosophical compass for those seeking simplicity without sacrifice, beauty without clutter and wellness without excess.

In design, lagom becomes a powerful guiding principle. It encourages us to create spaces that are functional, inviting and emotionally calming – never overdone, never barren. It is not minimalism for minimalism's sake, nor is it about achieving aesthetic perfection. Instead, it is about cultivating enough: enough room to breathe, enough comfort to enjoy, enough detail to spark quiet joy.

Bringing the spirit of lagom into your garden means designing with thoughtful balance, where every element has a purpose, but nothing feels excessive. Like the Japanese concept of ma, it's about embracing space as much as form, allowing areas to breathe and light to move freely.

Create soft, functional zones – a modest bench, a gentle path or a simple planting bed – ensuring smooth, intuitive transitions. Use a restrained palette of natural materials like stone, wood and greenery to keep the space calm and cohesive. Let nature take part in the design, welcoming the changes of light, shadow and season. In this way, your Japandi garden becomes a quiet, balanced reflection of life lived simply and well.

In a world that often leans towards more, lagom reminds us that enough is beautiful. In a Japandi garden, it becomes a quiet foundation – a way of designing that leaves room not just for nature, but also for peace, presence and meaning.

Japanese gardens

Maybe you have seen or been to a Japanese garden. Or even had the pleasure of visiting one in Japan. Traditional Japanese gardens have long been revered as sanctuaries where nature and human creativity converge. Rooted in centuries of tradition and philosophical thought, these gardens are a celebration of nature's impermanence, balance and understated beauty.

There is a stillness in traditional Japanese gardens that goes far beyond design. These spaces are not created to control nature, but to listen to it – to interpret its quiet language and reflect its essence in subtle, poetic ways.

Where Western gardens may seek to impress through abundance, Japanese gardens seek to soothe through restraint. Every stone, every patch of moss, every curve in the path is deliberate. Yet nothing feels forced. There is a natural flow, a sense that the garden was always meant to be this way.

It would probably come as no surprise that I could write a whole book purely about Japanese gardens and their elements. There are several historic garden styles in Japan, each with its own focus and function. When designing a Japandi garden, you can draw inspiration from any of them, depending on the space and mood you wish to create.

For now, I'd love to share a few different types of gardens and elements to give you some inspiration. That way, you can pick the things you love and incorporate them into your own garden or outdoor space.

Karesansui – the art of stillness and stone

The first type of garden I would love to mention is often called a 'Zen garden' in the West, but *Karesansui* translates literally to 'dry mountain and water'. Yet paradoxically, in these gardens, you'll rarely find flowing water. Instead, the elements of nature – rivers, oceans, islands, even waves – are symbolically represented using rocks, gravel, sand and moss.

The origins of Karesansui can be traced back to the Muromachi period (1336–1573) in Japan, a time when Zen Buddhism was flourishing among the Samurai class and cultural elite. Influenced by Chinese Song Dynasty ink paintings and Taoist philosophy, Japanese monks began creating gardens that echoed the monochromatic, minimalist landscapes depicted in scrolls. They transformed flat courtyards into contemplative vistas using only stone, sand and carefully raked gravel. The practice of raking the gravel into deliberate patterns, along with thoughtfully placed stones and austere simplicity, embodies wabi-sabi, the beauty of imperfection and impermanence, as well as the essence of ma, the mindful space between things.

Some of the most iconic examples, such as the garden at Ryōan-ji Temple in Kyoto, were designed not for walking, but for viewing from a single, fixed perspective – often from the veranda of a temple. These gardens became physical meditations: stripped of distraction, anchored in silence and entirely devoted to the inner world. Their timeless principles continue to influence modern minimalism and are deeply aligned with the Japandi spirit of calm simplicity.

How to incorporate Karesansui elements into your garden

You don't need a temple courtyard to introduce the spirit of a Karesansui garden into your space. Even a small corner on a balcony or a quiet nook in a larger garden can hold its meditative power. As well as the elements below, it's lovely to add a simple, low bench nearby – not for decoration, but as a space for quiet contemplation or tea.

- Gravel or raked sand area: choose a small section of your outdoor space to lay fine gravel or pale pebbles (beige/sand or grey tones work beautifully in Japandi style). Then rake it into flowing or circular patterns using a wooden or metal rake – these lines represent water, wind or rhythm. Re-raking the patterns can become a mindful ritual, like resetting your mental space.
- Feature stones as sculptural elements: first select a few natural stones or boulders with texture and character. Avoid symmetry; irregularity is key. Then position them with intention – as if they were islands in the sea or mountain peaks. A grouping of three often works best in Japanese composition. Note: in smaller spaces, a single striking stone on a bed of gravel can be enough.
- Minimal, textural planting: you can use moss (or low, soft ground cover if moss isn't practical in your climate) to soften edges and add an organic layer. Limit plant variety. Choose evergreens, architectural grasses or dwarf pines that hold structure and calmness year-round. And place plants in a way that looks natural, not overly styled – leave ma, space between elements, for room to breathe.

Tsukiyama – the garden of layers and landscape

Rooted in Japan's Heian period (794–1185), *Tsukiyama* gardens – meaning 'artificial hill' or 'constructed mountain' – represent one of the earliest and most influential expressions of Japanese landscape design. Inspired by the natural beauty of the Chinese landscapes revered by the aristocracy of the time, these gardens were crafted not as a place to simply see nature, but also to feel it within the safety and privacy of one's own home or estate.

Tsukiyama, often referred to as a 'hill garden', is a traditional Japanese garden style that creates a miniature, idealised landscape using gentle slopes, ponds, stones, bridges and plants. Unlike the dry minimalism of the Zen garden (Karesansui), Tsukiyama gardens aim to evoke the feeling of natural scenery – rolling hills, distant mountains or meandering rivers – within a small, curated space.

At its heart, Tsukiyama celebrates the art of illusion and storytelling through landscape. Designers use elevation, layering and perspective to mimic vast nature in a compact garden. This makes it an ideal inspiration for Japandi-style outdoor spaces that seek both tranquillity and subtle visual richness.

Tsukiyama gardens embody a philosophy of shakkei, or 'borrowed scenery', where surrounding landscapes – distant mountains, trees and even the sky – are subtly integrated into the garden's composition. This technique creates the illusion of vastness within confined space. Hills are gently sculpted from earth, winding paths are lined with carefully chosen stones, and tranquil ponds mirror the sky, drawing the eye and the mind beyond the garden's boundaries.

Where Karesansui gardens lean towards abstraction and spiritual meditation, Tsukiyama gardens celebrate narrative and realism. A meandering path might symbolize life's journey; a bridge may hint at crossing between realms; a small island may evoke immortality or paradise. Every element has symbolic and spatial intention.

Bringing Tsukiyama principles into Japandi outdoor living

Today, the poetic structure of Tsukiyama harmonises beautifully with the Japandi aesthetic, which values both simplicity and storytelling. Whether your outdoor space is expansive or modest, here's how to embrace the Tsukiyama spirit.

- Layer with intention: use layered planting to create soft depth – low moss or ground cover at the base, medium shrubs in the mid-section, and taller plants or trees to anchor the background. Allow space between each layer, inviting the eye to move gently through the garden.
- Shape the ground: even with a flat garden or terrace, small mounds of earth or raised beds can mimic natural elevation. These changes in level suggest distance and dimension, echoing the rolling hills of classical landscapes.
- Add a water element: a small pond, ceramic water bowl or reflective water feature introduces calm and movement. If space is tight, a container pond with floating plants like water lilies or lotuses can serve the same meditative function.
- Incorporate stone pathways and bridges: lay winding paths using irregular stone slabs or gravel. These not only guide movement, but also invite contemplation. A simple stone or wooden footbridge over a dry creek or pond can serve as both a design feature and a symbolic transition space.
- Frame views and create vistas: use fencing, bamboo screens or plant placement to frame select views – within or beyond your garden. A curated viewpoint encourages presence and slow looking (see more on page 44).

Water for wildlife: even the simplest water element, like a shallow bowl, bird bath, or gently dripping fountain, can transform your garden into a haven for birds and pollinators. Place it in a quiet, semi-shaded spot and refresh the water regularly. Birds will come not just to drink but also to bathe, bringing movement, sound, and life into your garden.

Chaniwa – the pathway to stillness

The *Chaniwa* evolved during the Momoyama period (late 16th century), particularly under the influence of tea masters like Sen no Rikyū, who championed the rustic, pared-down form of tea ceremony known as *wabi-cha*. Rejecting the ostentatious displays of earlier aristocratic tea practices, Rikyū emphasised simplicity, humility and direct engagement with nature. The tea garden reflected this shift. It became a threshold between spheres: the worldly and the sacred, the noisy and the still.

Often nestled within temple grounds or traditional homes, the Chaniwa, or tea garden, is a space designed not just for beauty, but also for ritual and quiet transition. Literally meaning 'tea garden', Chaniwa is the outdoor component of the Japanese tea ceremony (*chanoyu*), guiding guests from the outer world to the intimate interior of the *chashitsu*, or tea room.

Unlike other Japanese gardens designed for visual admiration or symbolic storytelling, the Chaniwa is deeply functional. Every stone, plant and basin is placed with care to facilitate the ceremonial experience. A path of stepping stones (*tobi-ishi*) leads guests through a shaded, natural setting, encouraging them to slow their pace and attune to the textures underfoot. Along the way, guests pause at a *tsukubai* – a low stone basin filled with water – to ritually cleanse their hands and mouth, a symbolic act of humility and purification before entering the tea space.

Chaniwa gardens embody the aesthetics of wabi-sabi and ma, celebrating the subtle, the seasonal and the imperfect. They are often shaded, moss covered and intentionally quiet – designed not to impress, but to soften the senses.

Implementing Chaniwa principles in Japandi garden design

To bring the spirit of Chaniwa into your Japandi-inspired garden, think beyond decoration and focus on creating a journey. The tea garden is not a static scene but a sequence of experiences designed to slow the mind and prepare the soul. Begin with a defined path. Like the tobi-ishi in a traditional tea garden, use stepping stones, gravel trails or wooden planks to guide movement. These paths should meander gently, encouraging a more mindful pace and fostering awareness of each step.

- Consider incorporating a modern interpretation of the tsukubai. This doesn't have to be a traditional stone basin – any simple, low water feature using natural materials can serve as a place for pause and symbolic renewal. Even a shallow bowl or minimal fountain, surrounded by moss or soft grasses, can evoke the same reverent atmosphere.
- In terms of layout and planting, honour the aesthetics of wabi-sabi by favouring asymmetry, aged textures and seasonal shifts. Let moss grow naturally, allow plants to age and weather gracefully, and choose native or climate-adapted species that evolve over time. Create shaded pockets using small trees or bamboo screens to invite introspection and quietude.
- Lighting should be subtle and minimal. Perhaps a few lantern-style fixtures or soft solar lights to guide the way at dusk, preserving the garden's mood of quiet retreat.
- Furniture, if included at all, should be low, understated and crafted from natural materials, blending seamlessly with the environment.

Ultimately, implementing Chaniwa principles in a Japandi outdoor space means crafting an experience that is felt rather than shown. It's about inviting visitors – or yourself – on a subtle transition from outer noise to inner stillness. A space where nature is not arranged to impress, but to awaken attention, gratitude and peace.

Roji – a journey through quiet intention

The *Roji*, or 'dewy path', is one of the most poetic and symbolic forms of Japanese garden design. Historically part of the Chaniwa or tea garden, the Roji serves as the approach to the chashitsu (tea house), guiding guests through a quiet, natural setting that prepares them mentally and spiritually for the tea ceremony. The term Roji suggests not only a physical path but also a mood – a sense of moisture, quietness and seasonal presence, like the feeling of walking along a shaded forest trail just after rainfall.

The origins of the Roji date back to the 16th century, also particularly under the influence of tea master Sen no Rikyū, who emphasised simplicity, humility and sensory awareness in the tea experience. In this context, the garden is not decorative but experiential. Every element – from the placement of stones to the rustle of bamboo – is there to slow time and awaken presence.

In traditional Japanese gardens, the Roji leads to the teahouse not with grandeur, but with humility and intention. It is a quiet transition space, designed to slow the pace, invite presence, and open the senses. Every element within it is chosen not for show, but for its ability to create stillness.

Stepping stones (*tobi-ishi*) are spaced deliberately, guiding the walker with slow, mindful steps. A low stone basin (*tsukubai*) invites symbolic purification – hands rinsed, distractions released – before entering the contemplative space beyond. Near it, a snow-viewing lantern (*yukimi-gata*) offers a soft, flickering glow that deepens the mood, especially in twilight or winter. Simple gates and fences, often made of weathered bamboo or wood, gently frame the experience without asserting themselves.

The textures of the Roji are quiet and grounding: moss underfoot, dappled light filtering through leaves, the vertical rhythm of bamboo, or the subtle form of evergreens. Nothing clamours for attention. Instead, the garden is built around silence, shadow, and the graceful wear of time. It's not ornamental – it's sensory and emotional.

You don't need a teahouse to bring this spirit into your own space. A small garden, courtyard, or balcony can hold the same sense of ritual. Begin with a simple path – stones, planks, or pavers – that invites slower movement. Add a water element, even a shallow bowl with leaves, to anchor the space in stillness. Use natural textures like gravel, bark, or soft plants such as ferns or thyme to ground the senses.

Thoughtfully placed lighting – a small lantern near a turn in the path or in a quiet corner – can create a gentle nighttime glow, extending the invitation to reflect even after dark. Let shadows fall where they may. Resist filling every inch. A Roji-inspired garden embraces negative space and avoids clutter, allowing emptiness and silence to do their quiet work.

Tsubo-niwa – the Japanese courtyard garden

The *Tsubo-niwa*, literally meaning 'one tsubo garden' (a *tsubo* is a traditional Japanese unit of area, roughly 3.3 square metres), is a small-scale garden typically nestled within the interior courtyards of traditional Japanese homes, shops and temples. Though modest in size, these gardens carry profound aesthetic and emotional weight, acting as living pauses within architectural space – breathing rooms for the senses and soul.

Historically, Tsubo-niwa emerged during the Edo period as a way to bring nature into dense urban environments. In Kyoto's *machiya* (traditional wooden townhouses), where buildings extended deep behind narrow street fronts, a courtyard garden was often the only direct access to sky and greenery. These spaces became sanctuaries of light, air and seasonal change – reminders of the outside world, harmonised with the stillness of the home.

Despite their size, Tsubo-niwa are never ornamental. Their purpose is quiet presence and sensory depth. Through careful placement of natural materials and the interplay of light and shadow, they invite reflection, create mood, and connect the inhabitant to the rhythm of nature.

A traditional Tsubo-niwa – the small inner courtyard garden of Japan – is a quiet world composed not of abundance, but of presence. Its elements are few, yet deeply intentional. Natural materials like stone, gravel, bamboo, moss, and aged wood are chosen for their ability to weather beautifully, holding the marks of time with grace. Planting is minimal and meaningful: a single maple, a few ferns, or a camellia may be all that is needed, selected not for show but for their seasonal rhythm and subtle texture. Water, even when space is limited, plays a key role – perhaps through a small tsukubai or the sound of dripping water – reminding us to pause and breathe. Lanterns and stepping stones provide quiet anchors, lending structure and gentle rhythm. And most importantly, the Tsubo-niwa is often viewed from within the home, framed by a doorway or window like a living scroll painting, changing softly with the seasons.

This courtyard spirit aligns seamlessly with Japandi design, where Scandinavian clarity meets Japanese mindfulness. Whether you have a central patio, a slim light well, or a corner balcony, the principles of the Tsubo-niwa remain the same. Think small, but think meaningful. A single sculptural rock, a patch of moss, and a graceful plant can say more than a crowded flowerbed. Let light become one of your materials – observe how it moves through the day, and use slatted wood, foliage, or grasses to filter and shape it. Leave space open. Resist the urge to fill every corner. This is a garden not of decoration, but of stillness.

From inside your home, look out and frame the garden as part of your living space. Let materials flow between indoors and out – wood, stone, neutral tones – blending boundaries and creating visual continuity. Even in a contemporary setting, a courtyard can serve as a pause between rooms, a moment of exhale during a busy day. It is a quiet invitation to slow down, to notice light and shadow, and to reconnect—true to the essence of both Japanese tradition and Japandi philosophy.

Scandinavian gardens

Scandinavian garden design is deeply rooted in the region's cultural and environmental context. The harsh climates, with long winters and brief summers, have shaped a gardening tradition that emphasises resilience, functionality and a profound connection to nature.

In the 17th and 18th centuries, formal gardens influenced by French and Italian styles emerged, particularly among the nobility. Notable examples include Frederiksberg Gardens in Denmark, established by King Frederick IV in the late 1690s. These gardens featured symmetrical layouts, terraces and water features, reflecting the grandeur of European aristocratic landscapes.

However, as Romanticism took hold in the 19th century, there was a shift towards more natural designs. Gardens began to embrace the native landscape, incorporating local flora and creating spaces that felt organic and unmanicured. This movement aligned with the Scandinavian ethos of living in harmony with nature.

The 20th century saw further evolution, with a focus on sustainability and minimalism. Influential figures like Carl Linnaeus, the Swedish botanist who formalized the modern system of naming organisms, also contributed to garden design.

Types of Scandinavian gardens

Scandinavian gardens are as varied as the landscapes they inhabit – from windswept coastal areas and dense forests to compact city plots and rolling countryside. Despite these differences, a common thread runs through them all: a deep respect for nature, a preference for simplicity, and an intuitive response to climate and light. I would love to share about some of the most characteristic types of Scandinavian gardens.

You might notice that I dedicate more words to Japanese than Scandinavian gardens. This doesn't say anything about the significance of both of them in Japandi (life)style. It's because traditional Japanese gardens have been formally developed and philosophically refined for over a thousand years. They're deeply intertwined with spirituality, art, and aesthetics – shaped by Zen Buddhism, Shinto, and cultural practices like tea ceremony, poetry, and calligraphy. As a result, every element in a Japanese garden is laden with symbolism, intention, and historical meaning. There are distinct styles (like karesansui, roji, and stroll gardens), each with formal rules and purposes. The gardens are considered high art as much as horticulture.

In contrast, traditional Scandinavian or Nordic gardens evolved from practical, agrarian roots. They emerged in a context of short growing seasons, harsh climates, and rural living. Rather than being aesthetic philosophies, they were working spaces – for growing food, herbs, and useful plants. Beauty was present, but informal and unintentional, arising from seasonal bloom, useful perennials, and the natural charm of stone, wood, and mossy earth.

That said, Scandinavian garden culture has its own quiet richness – rooted in the relationship to light, landscape, and the seasons. Its emotional depth comes through in its simplicity, its resilience, and its deep connection to place. As Nordic design evolved (especially in the 20th century), these rustic roots began to merge with modernist minimalism – creating a cleaner, more intentional garden aesthetic that shares a kinship with Japanese restraint.

In short: Japanese garden tradition is more extensive, symbolically dense, and formally developed, and Scandinavian garden tradition is simpler, more practical, and less codified—but still deeply meaningful in its relationship to nature and seasonality. That contrast is exactly what makes Japandi gardens so compelling: they blend the spiritual discipline of Japanese tradition with the earthy warmth and pragmatism of Nordic life.

Cottage gardens: rustic charm and functionality

Rooted in traditional rural life, Scandinavian cottage gardens blend beauty and practicality. They are informal, lush and slightly wild, reflecting a lived-in aesthetic that prioritises both nourishment and sensory delight. A typical Nordic cottage garden brims with hardy perennials such as lupins, delphiniums and peonies, interplanted with kitchen herbs like dill, chives and thyme. Vegetables are often grown in raised beds, flanked by berry bushes and fruit trees – particularly apples, pears and redcurrants, which thrive in the northern climate.

Paths meander rather than follow rigid lines, and fences are often built of natural wood or stone. These gardens invite pollinators, foster self-sufficiency, and offer a seasonal rhythm of planting, harvesting and quiet reflection. While rooted in the past, they remain popular for their warmth, biodiversity and emotional richness.

In the context of a Japandi garden, the cottage garden's legacy can be reinterpreted through a lens of quiet intention and balance. Instead of recreating its abundant layers exactly, we can distill its essence: a nurturing, lived-in space that honours seasonality and supports biodiversity. Edible plants – such as thyme, chives, or rhubarb – can be grown in low, simple beds or containers, their forms chosen to harmonise with surrounding textures. Hardy perennials like peonies or asters can be spaced mindfully, allowing room for air, shadow, and contrast. A single fruit tree – perhaps an espaliered apple or dwarf pear – can offer structure, yield, and seasonal change, much like a Japanese cherry or plum.

Natural materials such as untreated wood, woven willow, or rough-cut stone can create informal paths or low fencing that echo the rustic charm of Nordic tradition while maintaining Japandi restraint. Rather than filling every space, these materials frame negative space, giving breath to the garden's form. A bench tucked beside an herb bed or under a tree canopy invites pause – a subtle nod to the contemplative spirit found in both cottage and Japanese gardens. In this way, the traditional cottage garden becomes more than a nostalgic motif. Within the Japandi philosophy, it is transformed into a grounded, generous presence – less exuberant perhaps, but no less rich. It fosters connection to the land, encourages seasonal awareness, and bridges the past and present with humility and grace.

To make your cottage garden feel even more inviting, extend the warmth of the indoors outside. Add soft cushions, tablecloths, and plaids for cool evenings. A few lanterns, string lights, or candles on the table add glow and charm.

Modern minimalist gardens – clean lines and calm intent

Modern minimalist gardens in Nordic settings are deeply rooted in the region's design heritage. Influenced by Scandinavian design principles – form follows function, less is more – these outdoor spaces are carefully composed, with every element serving a clear purpose. While their appearance may feel contemporary, their principles trace back to early 20th-century Scandinavian modernism, which emerged as a response to industrialisation and excess. Designers and architects such as Alvar Aalto emphasised honest materials, human-scale design, and the seamless blending of indoor and outdoor life. The garden, like the home, was meant to be lived in simply but beautifully – with restraint, purpose, and care.

In this tradition, minimalist gardens express a refined simplicity. Every element has a reason for being – nothing is superfluous, nothing shouts. The layout is clean and composed, designed to offer mental clarity as much as visual appeal. Pathways and planting beds are often geometric or softly curved, balancing natural growth with structural lines.

The planting palette is typically restrained and architectural. You'll find a quiet rhythm of forms and textures: ornamental grasses, boxwood, silver-leaved ground covers and evergreens provide structure and texture without visual clutter. Plants are spaced deliberately, giving each one room to breathe, allowing light and shadow to animate their presence through the day.

Stone, concrete and pale timber are used to create patios, benches and retaining walls, often softened by moss or ferns. Furniture is low profile and often built in, integrating seamlessly into the layout.

Yet these gardens are not sterile. On the contrary, they heighten the presence of nature by offering it a stage. A single tree becomes a living sculpture. A cluster of grasses becomes a moving tapestry in the wind. Silence, space, and natural light are not empty, but active elements – encouraging stillness, reflection, and connection.

These gardens are not devoid of nature, but heighten its presence by giving it room to breathe. The emphasis is on proportion, natural light and serene contrasts. They are places of mental stillness and quiet sophistication, mirroring Japandi's emphasis on harmony and intentional design.

Wildlife gardens – fostering connection with nature

With increasing awareness of climate change and ecological fragility, many Scandinavian gardeners are embracing biodiversity-focused landscapes. Wildlife gardens, sometimes called *naturhager* in Norwegian, aim to mimic wild habitats and support pollinators, birds and beneficial insects.

These gardens rely on native and climate-resilient species like wild strawberries, cranesbill, Sedum, heather and juniper. Lawns may be replaced with wildflower meadows or left to grow freely. Natural ponds, birdhouses, bee hotels and deadwood piles are common features that enhance habitat value. Paths are often informal, meandering through pockets of dappled light and shifting seasonal blooms. The result may appear unkempt to the untrained eye, but in truth it reflects a careful balance: a space where nature is allowed to lead, and humans follow respectfully.

A wildlife garden may seem unkempt to the untrained eye, but it embodies a thoughtful balance: it invites both the wild and the domestic into the same quiet space. Here, beauty emerges from diversity, and seasonal change becomes an ever-present teacher. This type of garden aligns beautifully with the Japanese principle of wabi-sabi – a reverence for impermanence, irregularity, and the beauty of things as they are. In a Japandi garden, where Nordic humility meets Japanese mindfulness, wildlife gardening becomes more than a trend. It becomes a gentle act of restoration – of letting go of control, and inviting the wild back home.

'A Nordic garden feels like a quiet dialogue with the landscape. Pine trees, mosses, small sand dunes, stones and pebbles softened by the weather, and water surfaces reflecting the shifting light embody the region's climate, coastal elements and rhythms.'

Jonas Bjerre-Poulsen - architect MAA, photographer and partner at Norm Architects

Courtyard gardens – urban sanctuaries

Tucked behind apartment blocks or nestled between old townhouses, courtyard gardens – known traditionally as *gårdhaver* in Denmark and Norway – have long offered a sense of peace amid the bustle of urban life. Historically, these shared inner spaces were both practical and communal: places to dry laundry, store firewood, or grow herbs and vegetables.

In cities and towns across Scandinavia, where outdoor space is often limited, courtyard gardens provide private refuges. Inspired by traditional gårdhaver, modern versions use container planting, vertical gardens, trellises and reflective surfaces to amplify light and space. Ferns, grasses, potted trees and herbs thrive in sheltered conditions. Water features, candlelight and fire bowls add sensory layers – coolness, movement, warmth and sound. Even a small balcony can capture this atmosphere.

These spaces often become extensions of the living room: small tables for morning coffee, lounge chairs tucked into sun-drenched corners, wool blankets for chilly evenings. Courtyard gardens are proof that intimacy and beauty can coexist in tight quarters. They embody Japandi's ethos of merging indoors and outdoors, creating a seamless flow of comfort and mindfulness.

Traditionally, Scandinavian courtyard colour palettes were soft and sun-reflective – chalky whites, dusty greys, muted greens and earthy tones designed to brighten long winters and harmonise with ageing brick or stone walls. Today, these colours still resonate, especially when paired with natural textures: raw wood, ceramics, linen and slate.

When you have limited space, you can choose foldable furniture that you can store easily. Choosing materials that can stay outdoors is a good idea if you don't have (a lot of) storage.

The principles of Nordic garden design

In contrast, yet in perfect complement to the delicate intricacies of Japanese gardens, Scandinavian garden design is a celebration of clean lines, functional beauty and a profound respect for the natural environment. Rooted in the values of sustainability and simplicity, this approach to garden design transforms outdoor spaces into extensions of modern living.

Embracing minimalism

Much like its architectural counterpart, Scandinavian garden design is marked by a clear, uncluttered aesthetic. Gardens are crafted to reflect a sense of order and clarity, where every plant, stone and water feature is chosen not just for its beauty, but also for its ability to enhance the overall balance of the space.

Integration with nature

Scandinavian gardens prioritise a seamless integration with the surrounding landscape. Rather than imposing a rigid structure, these designs allow nature to dictate the rhythm of the space. Native plants, natural stone and organic forms work in concert to create a garden that feels both curated and effortlessly wild. Wood, stone and metal are commonly used, chosen for their durability and ability to weather gracefully. Reclaimed and upcycled materials are favoured, reflecting a commitment to sustainability.

Seasonal rhythm and light

The long, luminous days of Scandinavian summers and the introspective quiet of winter find their reflection in garden design. Outdoor spaces are conceived as living calendars, celebrating the transient beauty of each season. The interplay of light and shadow becomes a crucial design element, creating a dynamic ambience that shifts with the passing hours. Lanterns, string lights and LED path lights are used to create a cosy feel.

Sustainable and thoughtful craftsmanship

At the heart of Scandinavian design is a commitment to sustainability. Materials are selected not only for their aesthetic appeal but also for their durability and minimal environmental impact. The result is a garden that is not only beautiful but also built to withstand the test of time, echoing the enduring values of simplicity and functionality.

Functional spaces

Gardens are designed for year-round use, with features like saunas, hot tubs and fire pits providing warmth during colder months. Seating areas are strategically placed to capture sunlight and offer comfort, embracing all seasons.

Plant selection

Hardy, climate-adapted plants are essential. Conifers like pine and spruce provide structure, while perennials such as heather, potentilla and lilies add seasonal interest. Fruit trees and herbs are also common, offering both beauty and utility. There is more about plants in chapter 3, page 213.

Colour palette

A soothing colour scheme of whites, greys and earth tones is typical, with pops of colour provided by plants and accessories. This palette reflects the Scandinavian appreciation for light and simplicity. Scandinavian garden design is an invitation to experience nature in its most refined form – a blend of art and pragmatism that honours both the beauty of the natural world and the necessity of thoughtful, sustainable living. It stands as a modern interpretation of ancient values, where the environment is both a source of inspiration and a canvas for creative expression.

In conversation with Annika Zetterman, Scandinavian garden designer

Annika Zetterman's distinct gardens are characterised by a Nordic simplicity, functionality and grace. With a sensitivity to natural materials and a lifelong love of Nordic flora, her creations convey thought and meaning, with the natural landscape as an integral element. I'd like to share some bits of our conversation about Scandinavian gardens with you.

When you think of a typical Scandinavian garden, what comes to mind?
Delicacy. The Nordic region, landscape and gardens have an abundance of small and delicate flowers and plants, vast meadows with ornamental grasses and petite wildflowers. Likewise, you find delicate ground-cover plants in forests and alpine plants in mountain regions.

What are the most common elements of a typical Scandinavian garden?
Certain plants are timeless in any Nordic garden – for example, apple trees and Syringa. These create memories for many people – with its profound flowers and scent, Syringa marks the beginning of summer and especially the children's holidays. Very old varieties of apple trees give fruit all the way until winter. Sitting under an apple blossom tree and enjoying Grandma's apple pie are special moments. So adding plants with cultural heritage creates a strong sense of belonging and connection.

What advice would you give to bring that Scandinavian spirit to small gardens, courtyards or balconies?
First, select materials that resonate with the Nordics, such as wood and delicate plants: ferns, grasses and small, graceful perennials, shrubs and trees. Wood is a versatile material, light yet strong. Second, it's important to plan for seasonal interest, like early spring bulbs and autumn-coloured foliage, and also help wildlife find food and shelter. Then it's all about simplicity and functionality. Create a space with purpose, where hard landscaped areas are no larger than needed, and value quality over quantity as well as excellence in execution to ensure gardens that last. For balconies in particular, Scandinavians have a profound love of summertime pelargoniums, ideally in terracotta pots, as they're not only decorative but also drought tolerant.

How do you recommend balancing between the natural landscape and designed spaces?
Focus on the essential, give priority to carefully selected spaces and don't overwork the garden. The complex terrain and topography in the Nordics mean that parts of a garden benefit from being left untouched. These wild and natural landscape elements – bedrock, forest, pine trees and meadows – can be highly valuable in acting as a balance to the designed spaces.

Checklist: Embracing influence from Japan and Scandinavia

In this first chapter, we have journeyed through the philosophical underpinnings of Japandi, explored the contemplative landscapes of traditional Japanese gardens, and celebrated the clean, sustainable beauty of Scandinavian garden design. Together, these traditions offer a blueprint for creating outdoor spaces that are not just visually striking, but also deeply resonant – a living testament to the idea that when design is in harmony with nature, every element sings in quiet, elegant unison. Here's a checklist to create calm, balance and beauty through simplicity and natural design. I know this is probably hard, but don't feel the urge to check all the boxes. Apply only what feels good and fits into your space.

Natural materials

- ☐ Use wood (preferably untreated or aged) for furniture, fencing or decking
- ☐ Incorporate stone or gravel paths (e.g., pebbles, slate, granite)
- ☐ Choose ceramic or clay planters with organic forms
- ☐ Add woven or linen textiles for softness in cushions or throws

Organic shapes and textures

- ☐ Embrace asymmetry and imperfection (inspired by wabi-sabi)
- ☐ Include uneven stone steps or irregular wood-grain surfaces
- ☐ Layer textures – mix smooth (ceramic), coarse (wood) and soft (textiles)
- ☐ Let plants grow naturally, without over-pruning or strict form

Minimalism and decluttering

- ☐ Keep decor minimal – prioritise fewer, better-chosen objects
- ☐ Use hidden storage or baskets to keep clutter out of sight
- ☐ Apply the 80/20 rule: 80% clear space, 20% visible decor
- ☐ Group items in threes or odd numbers for visual harmony

Balance and harmony

- ☐ Create visual balance – between soft and hard, natural and handmade
- ☐ Use symmetry sparingly; balance more through weight and flow
- ☐ Connect the indoors and outdoors with similar materials and palettes
- ☐ Leave space between elements; let the design 'breathe'

Flow and movement

- ☐ Guide movement with simple stone or wood paths
- ☐ Create subtle transitions between zones (e.g., from patio to garden)
- ☐ Use screens or planting to define spaces without enclosing them
- ☐ Encourage a slow pace – design for walking, sitting, reflecting

Sustainability as standard

- ☐ Embrace the lagom principle: live within your means and within nature's means
- ☐ Use recycled or natural materials like stone, timber, gravel, hemp rope and linen
- ☐ Collect rainwater for irrigation or create a small greywater system
- ☐ Choose solar lighting or LED fixtures with timers to reduce waste

CHAPTER TWO

The building blocks of outdoor harmony

I'd like to begin this chapter by introducing the concept of *oubaitori*. The Japanese word 'oubaitori' is made up of four characters, each representing a different flowering tree: *sakura* (cherry blossom), *ume* (plum blossom), *momo* (peach blossom), and *tachibana* or *lee* (apricot blossom). While all of these trees bloom in spring, each does so in its own time, with its own distinct colour, shape and fragrance. They flourish according to their own unique rhythm, illustrating that growth and beauty do not follow a single path.

Oubaitori is a gentle reminder not to compare yourself to others, and instead to honour your own path, timing and nature. It celebrates individual beauty and quiet self-acceptance – a core value in Japanese thought.

Applying oubaitori to garden design means embracing diversity, avoiding perfectionism and creating space for uniqueness – not only in the layout, but also in how plants grow and how people experience the space. Choose plants for their character, not uniformity. Mix textures, bloom times and species that reflect different 'personalities'. Let some plants take the spotlight in spring, others in autumn.

A Japandi garden inspired by oubaitori doesn't need constant bloom, but rather thrives in a seasonal rhythm. It's about accepting imperfection in all its forms. Allow for natural ageing, weathering and irregularity. A mossy stone, twisted tree branch or crooked stepping stone is not a flaw; it's personality and gives warmth to the space. Create quiet corners, shaded benches or winding paths that allow visitors to interact with the garden in their own way and at their own pace. If you have a (small) space for it, let part of the garden grow a bit wild, or let a plant self-seed in unexpected places. Oubaitori honours what grows naturally.

Designing with purpose and peace

Personally, I think designing a Japandi-style garden begins not with the planting or furniture, but with looking at its flow: how the space breathes, moves and welcomes you in. At its core, layout is about intentional space planning that allows for balance, calm and beauty.

Drawing from both Japanese concepts like Ma and Scandinavian functionalism, layout is about experience. It's about moving through a garden the way you'd move through a poem – quietly, meaningfully and with ease. Of course, have in mind what you like to do in your garden and ensure that the space invites you to enjoy your garden the way you like, too.

In this section, I'm going to help you shape the layout of your outdoor space. Every space is unique – whether in size, shape or climate – and these elements all play a role in the design. I'll share tips, ideas and steps that you can apply to your own space. Just like with interior design, it's important to consider what truly suits your space and personal taste. To me, the most important thing is that you don't just copy something you've seen elsewhere. Let yourself be inspired, and dare to make it your own, even if it doesn't fit perfectly within the Japandi style.

Stepping stones to design the layout

I'd like to walk you through a practical guide to help you design the layout of your outdoor space. You're of course free to use it however you like, but I want to point out that there's a logic behind the order of the steps. So, for the best results, I recommend following them in sequence.

1. Observe first, design later

To get to know the space and what would fit the best, I'd advise spending time in your garden at different times of the day. Watch how the light shifts, where the wind moves, where sounds come from and how people naturally walk through the garden. Note where doors open, slopes occur or fences interrupt. It's also important to check the drainage in your garden. I once replaced some tiles with grass and gravel, only to notice that water started collecting on the grass. Apparently, the tiles had been slightly sloped, allowing water to trickle towards the drain in the alley – something I hadn't realised until I made the change. On top of this, it's important to measure your space.

2. Define the purpose of the space

Just like with indoor spaces – where you might define a sitting area, dining space, home office or play zone for the kids – outdoor spaces benefit from the same thoughtful approach. In the garden, ask yourself: Do I want a place for solitude, social gatherings, gardening or simply a beautiful view? As with interiors, consider the needs of everyone living in the home. Prioritise based on your lifestyle, practical needs and what the space allows. In Japandi style, it's better to have fewer, well-defined zones than many that are poorly used.

shower
spa
paving
deck
pergola
nature
terrace
waste

living
entrance
canopy
pond
lawn
kitchen
nature
terrace
driveway
stacked logs
gravel
vegetables
greenhouse
shed

3. Map the zones

Once you've considered the purpose(s) of your space, you can divide the garden into functional zones. For example, you might include a seating area, planting bed, pathway, cosy morning coffee spot or water feature. It's a lovely idea to choose plants with specific scents for different zones. For instance, jasmine works beautifully in a sheltered morning coffee corner, while thyme and rosemary are perfect near a barbecue nook – great for cooking and even for adding a sprig of rosemary to your summer cocktail.

Things to consider on a (small) balcony and small garden:

- Mount shelves or planters to layer greens at eye level.
- Use tall, narrow planters to add height without bulk.
- Add vertical design features, like climbing plants.
- Let climbing vines soften railings or trellises.
- Choose a mix of form and texture: a tall grass for movement, a trailing plant for softness, a sculptural bonsai or dwarf pine for presence.
- Foldable, modular or built-in seating works best to save space.
- Use pots with a consistent texture or colour to keep visual clutter low. Clay, dark ceramic or aged terracotta work beautifully.
- In a small garden, keep the view as open as possible by minimising visual 'clutter' and using reflective surfaces like water or light-toned gravel.

Things to consider in a big garden:

- Break the space into intimate pockets.
- Use meandering paths to create rhythm and discovery.
- Consider sightlines from various spots – create focal points like a sculptural tree, stone basin or lantern.

Print out a satellite view of your garden and mark any relevant features or considerations. Also, walk your sketch. Use sticks or string to mark out paths and zones on the ground and feel how they work in the actual space.

4. Plan movement

Decide how you should move through the space. Consider curves over straight lines, stepping stones over concrete.

5. Let negative space (Ma) breathe

Purposely leave space open. Don't rush to fill every corner with objects, certainly in small gardens. Stillness is part of the design.

6. Light and shadows

Take note of which areas receive the morning light – perfect for enjoying your coffee – and which are exposed to the harsher midday sun, where some shade from trees might be welcome. Also, observe where the space glows during golden hour. Consider how shadows play a role throughout the day, like the dappled patterns cast by tree leaves on your terrace. I explore this further in the section on natural and artificial light (page 195), where I share more about working with light and shadow.

7. Balance soft and hard surfaces

Mix natural materials like gravel, stone and wood with plant softness. Ensure pathways transition gently into beds or sitting areas. On page 157, I share more about materials and how to maintain them.

8. Keep transitions smooth

Use changes in texture, tone or elevation to mark a shift from one zone to another. It should feel like you're walking through rooms, not crossing borders. Using organic and round forms can make transitions smoother as well.

9. Think in layers, not just lines

Try to avoid a flat view from any one point. Nature rarely presents itself in rows – it offers depth, layers and moments of gentle surprise. When designing your garden, think like a landscape painter: create foreground, middle ground and background in every view. This approach adds dimension and rhythm, even to small spaces. I will share more about these three layers on page 237.

10. Leave room for change

Your garden is a living system that's always changing. Design with flexibility in mind to accommodate seasonal shifts and growing plants. Also, in my opinion, it's best to take your time and avoid rushing into making all your decisions at once.

Eikenheuvelpad

In conversation with Noël van Mierlo, garden designer

Noël van Mierlo's gardens have a certain flow that invites you to explore. I immediately noticed that he implements multiple elements linked to Japandi, like wabi-sabi and Ma. He created all the drawings in this book and shared many photos of his gardens as well. Here, I'd like to share some of the topics we talked about.

What does flow in a garden mean to you in practice?
For me, flow is about guiding attention, movement and rhythm – without ever forcing it. A garden should naturally invite you to explore. In practice, this might be a path that curves just enough to spark your curiosity, repeating plantings that gently draw your gaze deeper into the space, or a tree placed in just the right spot with a welcoming chair beneath it that makes you want to walk over and sit down.

Are there certain patterns or design principles that you find yourself returning to again and again in your gardens?
I aim to make my gardens adventurous, so that visitors naturally embark on a journey of discovery. As you walk through the garden, perspectives shift: meandering paths among the plants make you part of nature, while a floating bridge turns you into an observer. I am also drawn to asymmetry, as it feels more natural and alive. These transitions help visitors leave the worries of everyday life behind and find calm. I call it 'mindfulness in action' – the garden fulfils its essential role.

How do you balance structure – paths, terraces, water features – with softness – planting, textures, seasonal change?
Without structure, a garden quickly feels chaotic; without softness, it lacks soul. I like to work with strong, clear structures – paths, terraces, walls, hedges – that provide clarity and direction. I then soften this framework with loose, seasonal planting that shifts over time and allows the garden to breathe. A good way to think about it is that what's built by people is often bold and geometric, while nature flows freely. It's precisely this tension that makes a garden feel alive and layered.

Light plays a huge role in Nordic and Japanese design. How do you apply this to a garden setting?
I observe how light moves through the garden, both during the day and across the seasons. The positioning of terraces is often guided by the desire for sunlight or natural shade. Morning light can beautifully illuminate a tree, while evening light creates long, poetic shadows across a lawn or along a wall. I often favour trees with a transparent canopy, allowing light and shadow to play continuously throughout the garden.

Finally, Japandi gardens invite reflection and presence. What design choices do you make to create not just a functional garden, but also a place of stillness?

The foundation of true relaxation lies in the natural world. It is no coincidence that people turn to forest bathing, shinrin-yoku, or picture landscapes in their mind while meditating. I believe our own gardens can be the perfect gateway to this. They surround us where we live, where we feel safe, where we belong. In a world that is moving ever faster, gardens can become sanctuaries – spaces to slow down, to ground ourselves, and to rediscover the living world we are inseparably part of. By shaping gardens that are lush and layered, full of contrasts and subtle details – places to wander, to pause, to feel the seasons shift – they become immersive, inviting us to be fully present, to experience wonder and, in doing so, to reconnect with not only nature but also ourselves.

A place to wonder for kids

In both Scandinavian and Japanese cultures, nature plays a quiet yet profound role in how children grow, learn and connect to the world. From an early age, being outdoors is not an occasional treat – it's part of everyday life, shaping values of respect, independence and mindfulness that echo deeply in Japandi design philosophy.

In Scandinavia, the concept of friluftsliv (see page 50) is not reserved for adults seeking stillness outdoors and in the forest. Going outdoors is for all seasons and weather conditions. Forest schools and outdoor kindergartens (*barnehage* or *udeskole*) are common, encouraging children to climb trees, build dens and observe insects. There's a belief that fresh air, unstructured play and nature build both resilience and imagination.

Nature isn't sanitised – it's muddy, windy and sometimes uncomfortable. And that's the point. This early connection fosters a lifelong sense of stewardship and appreciation for the natural world, reflected in Scandinavian homes and gardens where indoor and outdoor life blend seamlessly.

In Japan, nature is seen as a teacher of impermanence, harmony and humility. From a young age, children are taught to notice the seasons: cherry blossoms in spring, cicadas in summer, fallen leaves in autumn and snow in winter. The school calendar and national traditions are deeply aligned with seasonal changes.

Shinrin-yoku is a modern practice rooted in ancient appreciation of nature, meaning 'forest bathing' or immersing oneself in the atmosphere of the woods to reduce stress and enhance well-being. It may be a term coined for adults, but the essence begins in childhood: being present with trees, sounds and stillness. Nature is not a playground to conquer but a space to observe and exist within. In rural areas and even in city parks, children are encouraged to notice small details – a mossy rock, crooked tree or trail of ants. This quiet attentiveness nurtures a sense of inner calm and respect for the living world.

Naturbarn (Scandinavian cultural concept) – 'children of nature'. In Scandinavia, children are raised close to nature and free to play outdoors in all weather, exploring with joy and confidence. In garden design this means adding playful, nature-based zones like logs to climb, rocks to jump between or edible plants to explore. Keep spaces low tech and sensory – sand, moss, water, wood. Encourage creative, unstructured interaction with nature that is not overly designed or restricted.

Designing a child-friendly corner

A child-friendly spot doesn't need to disrupt the garden's tranquility. In fact, it can deepen its sense of life and connection by inviting the next generation to engage with nature. Choose a spot with soft dappled shade – under a tree, beside tall grasses, or near a seating area where you can relax and supervise. The area should feel slightly enclosed and safe, while still visually connected to the rest of the garden.

A few things to keep in mind:

- Opt for natural, durable materials like wood, rope and stone. A sandpit bordered by smooth timber, a balance beam made from a fallen log or a handmade mud kitchen can all blend into your garden seamlessly while providing hours of creative, sensory play.
- Choose with play in mind, and remember that children are drawn to textures and smells. Add soft ornamental grasses for hiding, herbs like mint or lemon balm for sniffing and tasting, and robust, fast-growing plants like sunflowers or nasturtiums that kids can care for themselves. Raised beds or large pots can become their mini gardens. Be aware that some plants are toxic to children (and also to pets).
- Consider interactive elements, like large stepping stones, a chalkboard wall, or even a water feature like a shallow, recirculating stream (always be aware of water around your kids, especially when they are young) where they can splash about or float leaves. For quieter moments, include a child-sized hammock or a low wooden platform with floor cushions for reading or stargazing.
- Keep the palette and materials in tune with the rest of your garden. Use soft, muted tones, organic shapes and timeless textures. This makes the children's corner part of the whole, not separate from it.

Aesthetic and sensory – forms, shapes, materials, colours and textures

In the Japandi style, shapes, materials and textures are not just aesthetic choices, but also sensory experiences. True to both Japanese and Scandinavian values, forms are clean but not sterile, organic yet deliberate. Materials are celebrated for their natural origin, ageing process and tactile quality, creating outdoor spaces that feel both rooted and refined.

A Scandinavian word that beautifully captures this ethos and section is *ärlig*, meaning 'honest'. In Nordic culture, honesty isn't just about truthfulness in speech; it's also about authenticity in the things we surround ourselves with. An ärlig home, or garden, is built with materials that are true to their nature and designs that serve both function and feeling.

In this section, we explore how to apply this honesty – this ärlig sensibility – to your outdoor space. From organic forms that echo the natural landscape to untreated wood that weathers with grace, every element should feel grounded, tactile and real. Whether you're shaping a winding path, choosing stone for a wall or layering textures, the Japandi way reminds us: form follows feeling, and materials carry memory. Here, we let shapes speak softly and materials age gracefully – always in harmony with the rhythm of the outdoors.

Shapes – the silent architects of space

Shapes influence more than just aesthetics – they shape how we feel, move and experience a garden. They guide the eye along a path, signal where to pause or slow down, and offer rhythm and calm. In Japandi design, shapes aren't mere decoration; they're a quiet, powerful language that speaks through every element, from layout to planting, from furniture to containers.

I would love to share about shapes in Japandi outdoor design, starting with the traditions behind Japanese and Scandinavian approaches to form and shape. From Japan, we embrace organic, flowing forms – curves, asymmetry and shapes inspired by nature's imperfect beauty. These shapes create a sense of quiet movement and contemplative flow. From Scandinavia, we inherit a love for simplicity, clarity and functional geometry – rectangles, straight lines and clean edges that anchor and organise a space.

When thoughtfully combined, these two design languages form a harmonious whole: wild yet composed, soft yet grounded. The result is a layout that not only looks beautiful but also feels inherently right. A Japandi garden, after all, thrives on the balance of opposites, where form isn't mere ornamentation, but also a quiet expression of design intent. In the following pages, I explore the roots of shape in both Japanese and Scandinavian traditions.

'Today's outdoor spaces often merge these traditions, balancing richness and simplicity, but their enduring appeal lies in how they connect us to nature and memory.'

Jonas Bjerre-Poulsen - architect MAA, photographer and partner at Norm Architects

Japanese influences – shapes that flow with nature

Rooted in centuries-old philosophies like wabi-sabi and shizen (see pages 32 and 41), Japanese gardens rarely follow symmetrical layouts. Unlike Western traditions that often centre on perfect balance, Japanese design embraces asymmetry as a reflection of the natural world. An off-centre stone, a slightly tilted lantern or an uneven arrangement (mostly three or five) of trees suggests nature's spontaneity and encourages a slower, more mindful journey through the space. Asymmetry avoids predictability and stimulates curiosity. It gives the viewer the sense that the garden is never fully revealed in one glance, but unfolds gradually, just like a story.

Here, shape serves more than just function or beauty; it's a language of movement, meditation and meaning. Curving paths, unevenly spaced stones and irregularly shaped ponds are carefully arranged to feel organic – never accidental, yet never forced. This use of shape encourages exploration and invites quiet moments of reflection.

Historically, Japanese gardens developed around temples, tea houses and private residences, each with its own guiding philosophy (see chapter 1). Roji gardens, for instance, feature winding stone paths and water basins that prepare the mind for the tea ceremony. Zen gardens, or Karesansui, use raked gravel and strategically placed rocks to suggest vast landscapes within a confined space. In all of these, the shapes used – whether a round stone lantern, an arched tree branch or a softly mounded moss island – work in harmony with the land.

Crucially, Ma (see page 38) is treated as a shape in itself. Open areas of raked gravel or untouched soil are not empty – they offer contrast and breath. Just as a single branch might lean purposefully across a blank wall, shape in a Japanese garden is as much about restraint as it is about placement.

Scandinavian influences – shapes rooted in simplicity and function

In traditional Scandinavian gardens, shape has always been more than a matter of aesthetics. It also reflects a way of life influenced by climate, culture and a close relationship with nature. The long, dark winters and fleeting, light-filled summers of the Nordic region have led to an outdoor design philosophy that values clarity, durability and practicality. While minimalism is often associated with contemporary Scandinavian design, its origins stretch far deeper, grounded in centuries of resourcefulness and harmony with the land.

Historically, Scandinavian farmers and craftspeople approached their outdoor spaces with purpose. Gardens were laid out in logical, often geometric patterns to support both function and beauty. Rectangular vegetable plots and straight gravel paths weren't simply design choices – they were efficient, easy to maintain and adaptable to the changing seasons. This pragmatic approach created an understated visual order, with low wooden fences, modular planting beds and square terraces helping define space without overwhelming the natural surroundings.

These structured forms, often built from local, natural materials, brought rhythm to the landscape while remaining visually quiet. A rectangular bench placed along a path, a line of birch trees framing a lawn or box-shaped hedges enclosing a kitchen garden – all are examples of how geometric simplicity can work hand in hand with the organic irregularities of Nordic nature.

This tradition of shape in Scandinavian gardens continues to influence modern outdoor design. It encourages us to think in clear zones, to use symmetry for calm and to build with longevity in mind. In Japandi gardens, this sense of thoughtful order pairs beautifully with the Japanese appreciation for asymmetry and flow, creating spaces that are both structured and serene.

'Traditions evolve, but their essence remains powerful. The cottage garden celebrates biodiversity, abundance and intimacy – a reminder of our agrarian roots and love of diversity. The minimalist Nordic approach celebrates restraint, naturalness and clarity.'

Jonas Bjerre-Poulsen - architect MAA, photographer and partner at Norm Architects

The rule of thirds – quiet harmony through proportion

In both Japanese and Scandinavian aesthetics, balance is rarely achieved through perfect symmetry. One of the most timeless and effective tools for this is the rule of thirds – a principle borrowed from art and photography that can guide the layout of your garden, patio or balcony. The method resonates deeply with the principles of ma and lagom. It encourages thoughtful spacing, purposeful emptiness and visual rhythm.

How to apply the rule of thirds in your outdoor space

Imagine dividing your outdoor area into nine equal sections using two horizontal and two vertical lines – like a noughts and crosses grid. Most smartphones can show these lines when you're taking a photo.

The key idea is to position focal elements – like a tree, sculpture or bench – off-centre at one of the points where the lines intersect. This helps avoid a static or overly symmetrical layout and instead guides the eye through the space naturally and comfortably.

Rather than placing everything in the middle, shift elements slightly to one side. This creates a more relaxed, organic feel and enhances the sense of balance without being rigid.

This principle can also guide how you divide the space functionally, especially in small to medium-sized gardens. Try breaking it into thirds horizontally or vertically. One-third might be dedicated to planting, another to seating, and the last to open space or circulation.

Vertical thirds matter, too. When layering plants, think in levels: ground covers at the base, mid-height shrubs in the middle, and taller elements like grasses or trees at the top. This creates depth and prevents the space from feeling bottom or top heavy – see page 237 for more information.

Even on a narrow balcony, the rule of thirds applies. Think in vertical layers: a rug or tiles on the floor, seating in the middle zone, and climbing plants, hanging lights or privacy screens in the upper third. Group pots by height – tall ones at the back, medium in the middle and trailing plants at the front. Place furniture like a bench or chair along one-third of the floor area, not directly in the centre.

Use the rule of thirds as a starting point, not a strict formula. Let it help you guide the eye, create visual interest and achieve harmony – without over-planning. Nature loves a little imperfection.

Natural materials – honesty and warmth

It's no surprise that, just like in a Japandi interior, you'll find plenty of natural materials in a Japandi-style outdoor space. Exposure to the elements – like rain and sun – can cause these materials to age beautifully, but they also require a bit of care. Here are some simple maintenance tips to help keep everything looking its best.

Wood

Let me start with one of my favourite materials: wood. It instantly adds warmth to any space and plays a key role in both Japanese and Scandinavian design. Also, wood comes in many types and colours, so I'm sure there is one that fits your taste. In Japan, for example, you'll find materials like *Sugi* (Japanese cedar), *Kuri* (Japanese chestnut), *Hinoki* (Japanese cypress) and even bamboo – technically a grass, but often treated like wood in design.

In Scandinavia, historically, you find mostly light wood, like oak, pine and larch. It can be used for a lot of things, like benches, decking, fencing or planters. Its soft grain and warm tones invite touch and offer a subtle contrast to stone and foliage. Left untreated, wood can weather beautifully, taking on a silvery tone that suits both Japanese restraint and Scandinavian softness, telling the story of the seasons.

To help soft wood like pine or spruce last without compromising its natural look, you can treat with linseed oil, outdoor stain or weatherproof sealants once or twice a year. While many traditional Japanese woods are best suited for indoor or sheltered outdoor spaces, they can be used outside when properly treated with natural oils or by techniques like shō sugi ban (see page 160).

It's wise to elevate wood slightly above ground level to protect it from constant moisture and rot – an example of working with nature, not against it.

Shō sugi ban

One especially poetic method of wood preservation is *shō sugi ban*, a traditional Japanese technique that involves gently charring the wood to enhance its durability. Shō sugi ban, also known as *yakisugi*, is suitable for both inside and outside. Originally developed in the 18th century to weatherproof cedar siding, the method involves lightly burning the wood, cooling it, cleaning off the soot and then finishing it with natural oils. The result is a richly textured surface that resists water, insects and fire, while highlighting the grain with deep, matte black tones and silvery undertones.

This process darkens the grain, strengthens the surface and offers a rich, smoked finish that's both striking and sustainable. It's ideal for planter boxes, seating and even the outside of (garden)houses. As it weathers, the surface evolves beautifully, reflecting both age and intention.

Stone

Whether it's the rugged texture of granite, the smoothness of river stones or the sculptural presence of upright boulders, stone introduces grounding energy into the space. It can be used in paths, water basins, tables or focal points. Over time, stone may collect moss, especially in shady or damp spots, a natural evolution that adds to its character. Personally, I like moss, but if you don't or if it makes it slippery, a quick sweep or occasional rinse is often all it needs. A diluted vinegar solution can be used to remove any unwanted staining without the use of harsh chemicals.

Clay and ceramics

These materials reflect the human hand, bringing a deeply tactile presence, as seen in terracotta pots, handmade tiles and water bowls. While durable, they can be sensitive to frost, so it's best to bring certain ceramic items indoors during harsh winters or elevate them to prevent moisture accumulation at their base. Their porosity supports healthy roots and moisture balance. Accept cracks and patina as part of their natural evolution.

'Stone provides solidity, wood brings warmth and softness, water reflects its surroundings, accentuates weather conditions or introduces movement, and plants celebrate the changing seasons. The dialogue between these elements shapes the atmosphere of the garden – whether it is serene, wild or contemplative.'

Noël van Mierlo – garden designer

Metal

Metal in Japandi gardens mostly isn't flashy – it's humble and often weathered. Corten steel, for instance, is a favourite for planters, edging or screens; it develops a rich, rusted patina over time that blends effortlessly with earth and plant life. Rather than resisting the effects of weather, Japandi design embraces them. That said, if you prefer less change in colour or texture, a simple sealant can help preserve finishes on metals like iron or brass. And if you like shiny metal, it can add an extra layer in your space if the metal is placed intentionally to reflect a certain thing or view. In this way it creates a canvas.

Linen

Linen is a wonderful way to add a touch of softness to your garden. Use it for cushions in your lounge area or as tablecloths, runners or napkins to elevate your outdoor dining table. It can be wise to not expose linen to natural elements and store it in a dry place when not in use.

Ageing

Throughout all these choices, one philosophy remains constant: the beauty of imperfection and natural ageing. A cracked clay vessel, weathered wooden bench or moss-touched stone does not need to be 'fixed'. These are signs of life, time and use. In Japandi design, the goal is not to resist nature, but to collaborate with it. When natural materials are chosen with intention and cared for with respect, they do more than form the bones of your garden – they also help tell its story, season after season.

Colour palette – the poetry of earthy tones

In Japandi design, colour is not screaming loud; it's layered, muted and intentional. It is also not 'just' a palette of beige tones. This doesn't mean that if you love beige, go for it. Japandi's palette is formed by nature, reflecting the soft greys of stone, the warm hues of aged wood, the green of moss and the ever-shifting tones of the earth and the sky.

Before diving into the use of colour in Japandi style, I'd first like to briefly touch on the colour palettes of Japanese and Scandinavian design. This will help you better understand the blend that defines Japandi, and it also gives you the opportunity to lean more towards either a Japanese or Scandinavian feel in your space – whichever suits you best. That said, all tips and inspiration aside, the most important thing is that you feel happy with your space. Create a home that helps you recharge and brings you comfort.

Japanese colour tradition – inspired by Sanzo Wada

In Japanese design, colour is subtle, seasonal and steeped in meaning. This approach was beautifully captured by Sanzo Wada (1883–1967), a visionary artist, teacher and kimono designer who laid the foundation for modern colour theory in Japan. At a time of cultural transition during the early Shōwa period, Wada compiled *Haishoku Soukan* ('A dictionary of colour combinations'), a six-volume work (1933–1934) featuring 348 curated palettes. His colour combinations offered a quiet sophistication, blending tradition with a growing Western influence.

Wada believed that colour should not dominate, but harmonise. His palettes – drawn from nature, architecture, textiles and everyday life – show how carefully balanced hues can shape emotion, mood and clarity in a space. Be it earthy browns with muted indigo or pale moss greens paired with warm neutrals, each combination speaks with restraint and depth.

Historically, colours in Japan were often tied to nature, poetry or spiritual meaning. Soft mossy greens, weathered greys, burnt sienna, charcoal black and faded indigo are common in traditional architecture and garden design. These tones were developed from natural pigments and plant dyes, like indigo (*ai*), persimmon tannin (*kakishibu*), or the reddish-brown of beni extracted from safflower petals. Even the colour of a kimono or tea bowl once held layers of cultural significance, reflecting one's status, the season or a philosophical ideal.

In Japandi design, these traditions manifest through deep, grounding neutrals: dark-stained woods, subdued greens, muted reds and the occasional accent of seasonal colour – always with restraint, always with purpose.

ROOT
NURTURE
GROW

Scandinavian colour tradition – light, life and simplicity

In Scandinavia, light is the primary design consideration and colour choices are a response to the rhythm of northern seasons. With winters long, dark and snow-covered, Scandinavian design evolved to make the most of natural light. This has given rise to a colour tradition rooted in brightness, softness and minimal contrast.

Historically, the walls of farmhouses were painted white or pale yellow, interiors were lime washed, and furniture was left bare or painted in light blues, greys and muted greens – all chosen to reflect what little light was available. The natural tones of birch, pine and ash were celebrated, not covered, reinforcing a connection to the land and forest.

By the 20th century, Nordic modernism – championed by designers like Alvar Aalto and Arne Jacobsen – pushed this tradition further, embracing a restrained, functional palette. White became dominant, paired with soft greys, dusty pastels and gentle blues. The goal was not just aesthetics, but also well-being: colours that made small, often dim spaces feel open, fresh and alive.

Today, Scandinavian colour still leans towards cool, clean neutrals, but warmth is added through natural materials – blond woods, wool textiles and clay ceramics – ensuring the space remains inviting, not sterile. Nowadays you also see the influence of Japan in Scandinavian design and colour use.

'The gestures are subtle: muted colours, seasonal blooms, restrained compositions that leave space for silence.'

Jonas Bjerre-Poulsen - architect MAA, photographer and partner at Norm Architects

Nature as your colour palette

What I love about Japandi is how it blends two distinct design styles. It doesn't just invite you to embrace the look as a whole; it also gives you the freedom to lean more towards either the Japanese or Scandinavian influence, depending on what speaks to you most. Ultimately, I always encourage people to choose what they genuinely love.

While colours are often associated with certain moods or feelings, I believe the way colours make you feel is very personal. It depends on the kind of atmosphere you want to create in your home or garden. For example, my feelings about natural (especially bright) colours found in plants are different from how I experience those same colours when they appear in furniture or other materials.

For everything in your garden – except the living elements – the Japandi palette offers a grounded and calming foundation. There are no screaming colours here; this is a colour language that whispers rather than shouts. But as mentioned before, it's definitely not just beige. Think beyond linen tones: rich wood-inspired browns, deep blacks, warm terracotta, muted dark reds and mossy greens. In Japandi gardens, contrast is gentle rather than stark – used to add quiet interest without overwhelming the senses. This subtle layering is what gives Japandi gardens their emotional depth. The palette doesn't demand your attention, but rewards it, with harmony, softness and quiet strength revealed over time.

60–30–10

In my second book, *Japandi – Serene Homes and Thoughtful Living*, I wrote about the 60–30–10 colour rule for indoors, which I used to create my own lime paint collection together with Betonlook. But it can also be applied outdoors: 60% is the main colour (think gravel, deck, walls, large surfaces), 30% is the secondary earthy tones (planters, wood elements, larger plants) and 10% is accents (seasonal blooms, cushions, textiles and pots in deeper greens and even faded rust reds or indigo).

Don't forget trees, plants, and flowers in your colour palette. Many of them change over the seasons.

Furniture – stillness and simplicity

In Japandi outdoor design, furniture is more than a function – it's a quiet presence that invites rest, reflection, and connection to the outdoors. Whether it's a small city balcony or a spacious garden, furniture should feel purposeful and deeply integrated into the environment.

Traditional Japanese outdoor furnishings were often minimal and close to the ground. Think of *engawa* – the transitional wooden veranda – and low platforms for sitting or tea ceremonies. Symbolically, this furniture represents humility, being grounded, and a strong connection to nature. Scandinavian furniture evolved with a strong emphasis on functionality, durability and a warm minimalism. In gardens you'll find clean-lined benches, modular seating and wooden dining sets made from native timbers. There's also a cultural tradition of hygge, creating intimate, cosy moments outdoors even in cooler seasons.

'Materials are tactile and honest: pine, oak, natural stone, gravel paths. These elements together evoke a sense of legacy and resonance, celebrating the beauty of change and impermanence.'

Jonas Bjerre-Poulsen - architect MAA, photographer and partner at Norm Architects

Sitting area - grounded comfort

A Japandi-style sitting area is a space of quiet presence and grounded comfort. It invites you to pause, breathe and engage with the landscape slowly. Whether you're working with a compact balcony or a generous garden nook, the sitting area should feel visually balanced and gently integrated into its natural surroundings.

Japandi seating blends Japanese restraint with Scandinavian warmth – function and form in quiet harmony. Think low (wooden) benches, with or without backrests. These echo the traditional Japanese platforms used in engawa, but are often crafted with Scandinavian precision and natural joinery. Keep the silhouette low and minimal, allowing the surrounding plants or textures to remain the focus.

Floor cushions, *tatami*-style mats or woven stools introduce softness and flexibility and are ideal for smaller spaces or temporary layouts. Choose neutral-toned textiles in linen, hemp or recycled outdoor fabrics.

Daybeds and modular sofas are a great way to introduce a variety of shapes into your garden. If your space already features lots of clean, straight lines, consider softening things up with curved designs, and vice versa. Look for natural frames like oak, ash or powder-coated steel, and choose cushions in quiet, tactile fabrics. Think earthy taupes, stone greys, muted olive or soft black for a grounded, serene palette.

These days, there's also a wide range of outdoor furniture made from materials designed to withstand the elements. This is especially helpful if you don't have much storage space for cushions. Many modern outdoor sofas and chairs are not only weather resistant but also soft and comfortable. Personally, I love the look and practicality of these pieces.

Built-in seating is another hallmark of Japandi design, especially in smaller places. A low rendered wall or timber bench integrated into your hardscaping can double as a planter edge or subtle boundary. Let it serve multiple functions with elegant simplicity. For added charm, consider tiling the bench, perhaps with a beautiful single tile or two complementary tones. Just be sure to choose frost-resistant tiles and plaster.

When it comes to your coffee table, think about how you'll use it. If you often entertain and serve snacks, a larger table offers the space you need. You might also add a small side table – especially useful in a spacious seating area – so everyone has a convenient spot for drinks. A coffee table can also be a bold statement piece, so don't be afraid to get creative with its shape and colour. To stay true to Japandi principles, opt for a low-profile design.

Add pergolas or parasols where you need extra shade during the day, and consider a parasol that is easy to relocate if you don't have a lot of space.

You can anchor a sitting area with a textured rug, wooden deck tiles or a gravel base to define the space and soften transitions. Add one subtle focal object like a ceramic vessel, small fire bowl or lantern for visual grounding.

Dining area – understated gathering

A Japandi-style outdoor dining space is not about grandeur, but about essence. Eating outdoors becomes an intentional moment, shaped by modesty, presence and connection. Whether it's a long summer lunch, a quiet coffee at sunrise or a shared dinner under soft light, the setting supports a slower pace and a deeper experience.

From Japanese tea gardens, we inherit the idea that outdoor moments can be rituals and are deliberate, seasonal and deeply tied to nature. Think of a simple tea gathering under a tree or at a low table in a garden alcove, surrounded by asymmetry and stillness. In Scandinavian culture, the tradition of friluftsliv celebrates being outside in all seasons. From wooden terraces to fire-cooked meals, gathering outdoors is not a special event but a part of everyday life.

In the Japandi garden, these two worlds merge into a dining area that is warm, functional and timeless – designed for real life, not (just) a photo moment. When designing your dining area, it's helpful to consider how you plan to use it: for large dinner parties, casual breakfasts or everyday dinners.

Place the dining area in a semi-sheltered location like under a tree, next to a structure or beside a screen. This reflects the Japanese idea of *en* (framed experience) and provides comfort and cosiness. Allow space around the table. Don't overfill with pots or clutter. Let the open air be part of the experience, reflecting Scandinavian openness and Japanese Ma.

Japandi dining furniture is often crafted from natural materials, handmade or with visible joinery, and shaped to feel grounded yet inviting. You can go for clean-lined rectangular tables in solid wood or stone. Ash, oak or charred cedar (shō sugi ban; see page 160) are durable and age beautifully. It's also an elegant way to add organic and round shapes to your garden.

Especially in small or medium-sized gardens, a table can take up a significant amount of space in relation to the garden itself. Keep this in mind when choosing the shape and colour. A round or organic shape creates a softer look, and selecting colours similar to the surrounding ground helps the table blend in seamlessly.

Dining area - matching or complementing

When choosing seating, you can either go for a set that matches your table or find pieces that complement it well. If you decide on stools or chairs that differ from the table, it's important to check that their height works well with the table. While there are often standard heights, this isn't always the case, so measuring is key. If you need to store the chairs, stackable options can be very handy. Also, if storage space is limited, consider stools without separate cushions to save room.

With these practical considerations in mind, you can then focus on the design. A matching set of table and chairs creates a calm, cohesive look. Personally, I prefer mixing different pieces that complement each other in shape and colour, which adds a bit more playfulness. For example, you might choose a table with a surface in the same colour as the chair legs, and table legs that match the chair seats. While I appreciate good design, I believe comfort should always come first – especially if you enjoy long, relaxed meals.

For small spaces, a compact, foldable bistro set in muted tones can work beautifully within a Japandi style, especially when materials and shapes are thoughtfully chosen. Powder-coated steel, treated acacia or light bamboo all fit nicely in this palette. You might also consider a fold-down table that can be expanded when needed.

A Japandi dining space is where the landscape and daily life meet. It's quiet but generous, designed for connection between people, food and the natural world. Let each element serve a purpose: to hold, to host, to pause. And let the beauty come not from what's added, but from what's allowed to remain simple.

Light – shaping atmosphere and experience

In Japandi gardens, light is more than a practical necessity – it is a vital design element that shapes atmosphere, emotion and the rhythm of outdoor life. Both Japanese and Scandinavian traditions hold a deep respect for light, not only for how it illuminates but also for how it softens, highlights and transforms a space throughout the day and across the seasons. Whether it's the morning sun filtering through slatted wood or the quiet glow of a lantern near your evening bench, light in all its forms becomes part of the garden's living story.

Natural light and shadows

Natural sunlight breathes life into a garden. It feeds plants, creates shadows and adds subtle movement. The detailed effect of sunlight on plant health is discussed in the following chapter. It's helpful to observe your garden at different times of day and understand the sun's path. Notice which areas catch morning warmth, where shadows fall and how the light reflects off surfaces. These subtle patterns should inform where to place furniture, plants and focal points.

When designing your garden, creating shade is a way to create intimacy and offer protection from the sun when needed. One of the most elegant ways to create shade is by using plants and trees. Living shade adds biodiversity and a softness that feels both natural and timeless. To give it structure and guidance, you can make a pergola, and if the plant doesn't create enough shadow, you can also add a shade cloth or bamboo screens. Potted plants like tall bamboo or grasses in staggered heights can form gentle privacy screens and shade on balconies. Groupings can create intimacy while still allowing airflow and light play.

When natural shading isn't enough or possible – especially on balconies or open terraces – designed shading can be a seamless solution. Opt for green, red, beige or (soft) brown parasols, wooden pergolas with climbing plants or even movable shade sails in earthy tones. The aim is not to block the light, but to soften it, letting spaces breathe without glare.

Fire

An amazing form of natural light is fire. This can be a bonfire, where you gather around, enjoy a drink, and roast marshmallows. Or fire torches placed along a garden path, or even the gentle glow of a single candle.

In Scandinavian gardens, fire holds both symbolic and practical meaning, deeply rooted in cultural traditions shaped by long winters, short summers, and a strong connection to the natural world. Unlike Japanese gardens, where fire often appears in a more symbolic or ritual sense, in Nordic landscapes fire is directly experienced - bringing light, warmth, and togetherness into outdoor life.

Traditionally, bonfires marked seasonal transitions such as midsummer celebrations, when communities would gather to dance, sing, and honour the light. In winter, the hearth and open flames became central to survival and social life, offering comfort against the darkness. Today, this tradition continues in smaller, more personal ways: fire bowls, lanterns, and clusters of candles extend the day, turning even a chilly evening into an opportunity for connection.

Integrating fire into your garden does not always require large installations. A portable fire pit, a row of simple lanterns, or storm candles placed on a table can create intimacy and atmosphere. Fire has the power to transform outdoor spaces, reminding us of life's essential rhythms - light and dark, warmth and cold, solitude and community. It is a timeless element that ties modern Scandinavian living to its roots, while inviting a sense of ritual and presence into everyday moments.

Artificial light

Designing with both natural and artificial light allows you to extend the usability of your outdoor space while maintaining a soulful connection to time, season and shadow. Evenings in the garden invite a shift in tone. Artificial lighting plays a crucial role in Japandi outdoor living – not just for visibility, but also for creating mood and structure after dark. In Japandi gardens, light isn't static; it changes, dances, deepens.

There are three kinds of artificial lights to consider while designing your garden or balcony. Whenever possible, choose dimmable lights, because light without dimming is like music without volume.

- Ambient or cosy light. Think soft string lights, low lanterns or wall-mounted sconces with warm bulbs. These lights set a welcoming tone and encourage slow, mindful use of the garden in the evening. Hanging lights, like a few carefully placed paper lanterns, glass or linen pendants, or minimalist pendant bulbs, can create a floating canopy of calm.
- Accent lighting. Use soft directional spotlights or up-lighting placed at ground level to highlight a tree trunk, textured wall or sculptural stone. These lights create focal points and celebrate the garden's natural features.
- Functional lighting. Path lights, stair lights or low bollards ensure safe movement while still blending into the garden's calm aesthetic. Choose fixtures with soft, downward lighting to avoid harsh glare. Think solar spikes, small bollards or lantern-style ground lights.

When choosing artificial lighting, prioritize warm colour temperatures (around 2,700–3,000 K) to preserve the natural, serene feel. The glow should resemble candlelight or the golden hour rather than clinical white. Also mix electric and flame: candles in glass holders, tabletop fire bowls or small garden torches create emotional warmth no bulb can replace.

Rechargeable lanterns or small candle-style lamps add cosiness. Also, the portable function makes them very practical and lovely to use in several places in the garden.

Artificial light can interfere with animals' ability to sleep, reproduce, forage, migrate and communicate, ultimately affecting their survival and reproductive success. Take wildlife into account and use timers or turn off artificial lights at night.

Bridging the gap between indoors and outdoors

In Japandi design, the boundary between home and garden is not rigid, but a gentle transition. Both Japanese and Scandinavian traditions emphasise living close to nature. The goal is not to 'go outside', but to flow between indoors and outdoors with ease and harmony.

A window view becomes part of the garden. A potted tree on the balcony echoes one in the living room. Textures, tones and materials repeat – linen curtains, oak benches, slate stone and pale ceramics linking both worlds.

Here are a few tips to help you blend the boundary from inside to outside:

- Unify your palette: use similar colours and materials inside and out – neutral tones, softwoods, muted greens and stone greys.
- Frame views: position outdoor elements (a tree, lantern or water bowl) to be seen from key spots indoors – like the kitchen window or dining table.
- Flow with flooring: use continuous or complementary surfaces, such as indoor oak leading to outdoor larch decking, or tiles that run across thresholds.
- Soften thresholds: sheer curtains, bamboo blinds or sliding glass doors allow light and air to move freely.
- Extend living spaces: a bench just outside the door, a reading chair near a garden window – these gestures expand the sense of space.

In conversation with Jonas Bjerre-Poulsen, architect MAA, photographer and partner at Norm Architects

For this book, I explored how architects approach the delicate boundary between inside and outside. I really like the design approach of Norm Architects and already shared lots of stunning indoor spaces created by them in my previous two books. I would love to share a part of my conversation with Jonas Bjerre-Poulsen.

How would you perceive the relationship between indoor and outdoor space in architecture?

The design approach of Norm Architects, soft minimalism, is that the boundary between indoor and outdoor space is never a strict division but a conversation. Architecture becomes a frame for experiencing nature, not an obstacle to it. When surfaces, levels and materials flow seamlessly between the interior and exterior, the home feels like an extension of the landscape and the landscape an extension of manmade space. This continuity mirrors our evolutionary preference for open, safe yet stimulating environments – spaces where shelter and exposure coexist. It is not just about aesthetics, but also about well-being. Humans are biologically attuned to natural rhythms, light and textures, so a space that dissolves its walls strengthens our innate sense of calm and a connection to our primordial home – nature.

Can the use of natural materials create a more seamless sense of continuity between the two worlds?

Wood, stone, clay and other tactile, honest natural materials act as mediators between us and the shifting world outside. Their subtle imperfections, textures and ability to patinate over time resonate with the idea of nature as a living presence. When you use the same stone floor inside and on the terrace, or extend wooden cladding from the facade to the interior, you blur the threshold. These materials become a language of familiarity, grounding people and evoking the continuity of the landscape. Soft minimalism emphasises authenticity: materials that age gracefully, echoing the cycles of nature and reminding us that nothing is static, creating a symbolic connection to the living world.

Personally, I think it's different when you live in a small urban space. What are some simple ways to create a meaningful link with the outdoors for those spaces?

Even in a compact apartment, a meaningful dialogue with nature is possible. Small gestures, like a deep windowsill transformed into a green ledge, a sliding door opening onto a balcony with potted herbs, or a palette of natural tones and textures in the home, can make a space feel larger and more alive. Evolutionary psychology shows our stress levels drop when we encounter greenery and natural patterns, even in small doses. Light becomes essential: frame a view, amplify daylight, or mirror seasonal shifts with subtle interior changes. A few carefully chosen plants or natural materials can evoke the same biophilic response as a larger garden.

What would be your advice for someone wishing to blur the lines between inside and outside?

Think of continuity. Treat thresholds not as boundaries but as invitations to connect. Align floor levels, carry materials across zones, and create sightlines that lead the eye beyond the walls, borrowing landscapes on the horizon. Sliding or folding openings, sheltered terraces, and even furniture that feels at home both inside and outside strengthen this fluidity. And always listen to the context: let the local landscape, light and climate shape your decisions. When the built environment respects nature, the result is harmony, not contrast.

CHAPTER THREE

The living layer

Choosing plants and trees for your garden isn't just about aesthetics; it's also about balance between structure and softness, biodiversity and simplicity, wildness and design. Plants bring texture, height, movement and seasonal rhythm. From sculptural pines to swaying grasses, each plant contributes to the sense of quiet, balanced harmony.

But of course it's also about playfulness, so choose plants that you find pretty and fit in the climate you live in. It's also important to consider how much time you have or want to spend in the garden. Some plants are more needy than others, and no one likes looking at sad, droopy plants.

Whether you are tending to a few clay pots on a shaded balcony or designing a multi-layered planting bed in open soil, Japandi planting is guided by the same principles: intention, restraint and harmony. Plants should feel rooted in place – connected to the earth and in dialogue with their surroundings, not imposed upon them. This chapter offers information, practical tips and inspiration to create your own outdoor sanctuary where you can relax and enjoy nature.

Soil – the engine of your outdoor space

Choosing plants begins with the ground beneath your feet. Soil is more than just dirt – it's the quiet engine of your outdoor space, shaping what can grow and how plants will thrive. Maybe you live in Japan or Scandinavia? Then lots of typical trees, plants and flowers will probably work well with your type of soil. But if you live in a place with a totally different climate, it may be a bit harder.

Understanding your local soil type is key to creating a garden that feels effortless, grounded and naturally abundant. I'd love to share some common soil types with you, but be sure to check locally first, as this will make your planting experience much easier. Most local growers and garden centres are great resources to help you with this.

Sandy soils

Light, loose and well-draining, sandy soils warm up quickly in spring but tend to dry out fast. They are perfect for drought-tolerant plants such as lavender, thyme, ornamental grasses and Sedum. To improve moisture retention, enrich sandy soil with compost or leaf mould. Sandy soil pairs beautifully with the minimalist, sun-drenched palette of a Scandinavian coastal garden or a dry-style Japanese rock garden.

Clay soils

Heavy and moisture-retentive, clay soils are often nutrient-rich but can compact easily, making drainage a challenge. They benefit from regular loosening and the addition of organic matter. Choose plants that enjoy steady moisture, like ferns, astilbe, dogwoods, hydrangeas or Japanese iris. Avoid walking on clay soil when wet – it compacts quickly. Raised paths or stepping stones can help preserve its structure.

Loamy soils

This is the gardener's dream – well balanced in texture and fertility, loamy soils support a wide variety of plants with minimal intervention. If you're lucky enough to have loam, you can experiment freely while still embracing Japandi restraint.

Improving soil

Not all gardens have ideal soil, so my advice is not to aim to drastically change your soil type. Learn about its rhythm and match your plant choices to its qualities. A Japandi approach aims not for control of nature but for respectful cooperation. It's about working with nature rather than against it. However, there are some tips to improve soil health slowly and mindfully.

- Add compost yearly to increase the fertility and moisture balance. Use mulch (like bark, straw or leaf litter) to reduce evaporation and feed the soil life beneath.
- Encourage soil structure through (almost) no-dig gardening, letting worms and roots do the work. If your soil remains inhospitable, opt for raised beds filled with a custom blend of compost and soil.
- You can also plant in containers where you have complete control over the growing medium.

Plant traditions – roots in Japanese and Nordic history

Learning about planting traditions of Japan and Scandinavia can bring deeper intention to your garden. It connects you to centuries of cultural practice, natural rhythm and quiet design wisdom. While one tradition grew in lush mountain forests and the other in windswept meadows and coastal pine groves, both hold a deep respect for nature's presence, resilience and impermanence.

In Japan, planting has long been an art form intertwined with philosophy and spirituality. Gardens are designed to reflect the changing seasons, with plants like cherry blossoms (sakura) celebrating the fleeting beauty of spring and pines symbolising longevity and endurance. Moss is cherished for its softness and association with age and tranquillity, while maples bring dramatic autumn colour that invites you to reflect on impermanence. Each plant is chosen with meaning, creating landscapes that are as much about feeling as they are about form.

In Scandinavia, planting traditions have been shaped by survival and a strong connection to the natural landscape. The short, intense summers gave rise to a culture of celebrating seasonal abundance – apple trees, berry bushes, lilacs, and midsummer flowers like daisies and buttercups are all deeply symbolic. They evoke memories of harvests, festivals and family gatherings. Many of these plants, such as old apple varieties and hardy perennials, have been passed down for generations, linking gardens to heritage and resilience.

Japanese planting

In Japanese tradition, gardens are not just places of beauty and spaces of reflection but mirrors of life's impermanence and quiet depth. As early as the Heian period (794–1185), cherry blossoms (sakura) inspired poetry and symbolised the fleeting nature of life, a central idea in wabi-sabi, the appreciation of imperfection and transience.

With the rise of Zen Buddhism in the 13th century, gardens became meditative spaces. Plants were chosen for their spiritual resonance rather than their decorative appeal. Moss was treasured for its stillness and age, pine trees for endurance and bamboo for resilience. The practice of *bonsai*, drawn from Chinese *penjing*, reflected a desire to capture the essence of nature in miniature. Meanwhile, the concept of shakkei (see page 44) used plants to frame distant views, blending gardens and landscape into one.

Japanese planting traditions are steeped in symbolism. Each plant carries meaning: cherry trees express impermanence and stand for oubaitori (see page 113), pines stand for strength and bamboo for flexibility. Rather than bold colours or rigid arrangements, Japanese gardens favour subtlety and asymmetry. Trees lean gently, shrubs mimic the forest floor and moss softens hard edges – natural, unforced and full of quiet intention.

As previously mentioned, seasonality is essential. The garden shifts gently through the year: fresh green shoots in spring, vivid maples in autumn and sculptural forms in winter. These changes invite reflection and reinforce a connection to nature's cycles.

Among iconic Japanese plants are Acer palmatum (Japanese maple) for autumn colour, Pinus thunbergii and Pinus mugo for structure, bamboo for movement and moss for grounding calm. Seasonal highlights like camellia, azalea and wisteria offer delicate moments of bloom – never overwhelming, always meaningful.

At its heart, Japanese planting is not about display but presence. A Japandi garden borrows from this quiet tradition: layered, intentional and deeply alive.

Nordic planting

In the Nordic world, nature is not something to be mastered, but something to live with. The Scandinavian planting tradition is shaped by long winters, cool summers and a deeply rooted cultural respect for the land. It is quiet, honest and enduring. Where Japanese gardens speak in metaphor and poetry, Scandinavian gardens speak in modesty and trust – trust in the seasons, in function and in the subtle beauty of the native landscape.

Gardens in the Nordic region have long been extensions of practical life: places to grow food, gather herbs and seek sunlight. Yet they have always offered quiet beauty. The palette is restrained, favouring soft greens, pale blossoms, and earthy browns and greys. Plants are not overly curated, but rather chosen for their resilience, their simplicity, and their ability to harmonize with rock, wood and weather.

Birch, pine and spruce offer vertical structure and a sense of permanence. Shrubs like Amelanchier (juneberry), Viburnum and Rosa rugosa provide seasonal interest – spring blossoms, summer foliage, autumn colour and even berries in winter. Hardy perennials like Astrantia, Sedum and Achillea thrive in tough conditions and bring gentle, natural colour to the garden without demanding attention.

Grasses play an essential role. Genuses such as Deschampsia, Molinia and Festuca add softness and movement, catching the low Nordic light in the early morning and at dusk. Ground covers like moss and lichen settle between stones and timber, lending a timeless quality to even the newest garden paths.

Rather than relying on bold forms or symmetry, Scandinavian gardens often follow the existing contours of the land. Borders are softened, edges are blurred, and native wildflowers are welcomed for their biodiversity and ecological value. This natural approach fosters habitats for birds, pollinators and beneficial insects – making the garden not just beautiful, but also alive.

Scandinavian planting is also deeply seasonal. Light and shadow shift dramatically across the year, and the garden reflects that rhythm: the early green of birch leaves in spring, the fullness of summer grasses, the golden hush of autumn and the stark structure of evergreens in snow. There is beauty in every phase, and the design trusts nature to carry the story forward.

At its heart, Scandinavian planting is about quiet endurance and honest connection. It celebrates what is already there. When paired with the poetic intentionality of Japanese design, the result in Japandi gardens is a planting style that feels both timeless and grounded: rooted in place, rich with presence and beautifully alive across the seasons.

Choosing plants – seasonality and biodiversity

In this section, we dive a little deeper into creating biodiversity in your garden: how to attract insects, support a healthy ecosystem and choose plants with seasonality in mind so there's something happening all year round.

Let's start with seasonality. In a Japandi garden, seasonality is not just a backdrop but is the story itself. The garden shifts with the year: from fresh awakenings to quiet dormancy, each phase brings texture, emotion and rhythm. By planting with the seasons in mind, you create an outdoor space that evolves with time – never static, always gently changing.

Seasonal planting isn't about constant bloom. It's about tuning in to nature's tempo. The garden becomes a living reflection of impermanence and renewal – echoing the Japanese reverence for wabi-sabi and the Nordic love for life lived in cycles. Even in stillness, something is always happening.

Spring emerges softly. Early bulbs like tulips, alliums and narcissus bring gentle colour, while flowering trees such as Cornus kousa, Prunus incisa and Magnolia kobus offer sculptural blooms that feel like quiet celebrations. It's a season of promise, of subtle energy beginning to rise. It can be lovely to place bulbs in 'odd' places to give an unintentional and playful feeling to your garden.

Summer is a time of fullness and grace. Ornamental grasses (Miscanthus, Stipa), flowering perennials like lavender, Alchemilla mollis and Japanese anemones create a layered sense of softness and movement. These plants invite pollinators, echoing the Japanese appreciation of fleeting beauty and the Scandinavian delight in light-filled days.

Autumn brings a deepening. Leaves shift to russet, ochre and fire. Acer palmatum, Amelanchier and Betula add richness and structure. Hydrangeas fade with elegance. Seed heads and tall grasses are left standing, catching the frost and casting long, golden shadows. The garden leans in to memory and reflection.

Winter pares everything back. Now, form and structure speak the loudest. Evergreens like Buxus, Ilex and Pinus mugo provide quiet anchors. The pale bark of Betula utilis glows against bare ground. Dried grasses and spent flower heads add texture and silhouette – reminders that beauty persists in stillness.

Biodiversity in your garden

Designing with biodiversity in mind not only supports the environment, but also brings depth, movement and resilience to your garden. Even small gardens and balconies can support biodiversity. One vessel of lavender or thyme is enough to welcome pollinators. When you group insect-friendly plants in clusters, their attractiveness increases.

If you're aiming for biodiversity, it's helpful to have the following three things in mind when selecting your plants. First, choose pollinator-friendly plants that attract bees, butterflies and hoverflies. Second, select native species, adapted to your climate and beneficial to local wildlife. And last, choose multi-season blooms: by overlapping flowering periods you support insects year-round. There are a few key plant types that are really helpful for biodiversity. When you select your plants, check if they fit in the climate and with the soil type of your garden; otherwise look for an alternative with the same benefits.

Function	*Examples*	*Benefit*
Pollinator magnets	Echinacea, lavender, yarrow, alliums	Attract bees and butterflies
Berry producers	Viburnum, Amelanchier, elderberry	Feed birds in autumn/winter
Host plants	Grasses, nettles, native perennials	Support insect larvae and moths
Night bloomers	Evening primrose, white campion	Feed nocturnal pollinators like moths

South facing: Gets sun all day. Ideal for sun-loving plants, herbs and gathering zones. Consider adding pergolas or shade for comfort.

North facing: Cooler and shadier. Great for moss, ferns and hostas, and for creating a meditative, lush atmosphere.

East facing: Morning sun, afternoon shade. Perfect for a breakfast corner or soft, early-blooming flowers.

West facing: Receives strong afternoon sun, making it perfect for evening use. Ideal for cosy seating areas and enjoying golden-hour light.

Arranging your plants – height, layers and grouping

In nature, plants never grow in neat, single rows – they layer, lean, spill and rise with time and space. Recreating this natural layering in your Japandi garden introduces a sense of depth, softness and natural harmony. It makes the garden feel immersive, inviting exploration from every angle while guiding the eye gently through space.

To keep the garden visually balanced year-round, combine deciduous and evergreen plants. In every layer – ground, middle and structural – include species that carry texture and presence through the cold months. This way, even in winter, your garden will feel alive with quiet strength and form. It's also a beautiful way to add privacy and intimacy to your garden.

Planting in a Japandi garden is not just a surface activity – it's also a sculptural art. Think of your outdoor space as a three-dimensional canvas. Just as a good painting uses foreground, middle ground and background to create atmosphere, your planting should do the same. Your foreground is the ground layer (0–30 cm), the middle ground the middle layer (30–80 cm) and the background your structural layer (80 cm–2 m+).

Ground layer (0–30 cm)

This is the soft base of your planting. This is the closest to the earth, where subtle textures, softness and ground-hugging forms dominate. Think of it as the carpet of your outdoor room. Use creeping thyme, moss, dwarf mondo grass or Sedum. These plants hug the ground, fill gaps and soften edges and are ideal around stepping stones, under benches or along the base of planters. Visually grounding and often fragrant or tactile, this layer invites you to pause and notice details.

Middle layer (30–80 cm)

This layer provides volume and visual rhythm, acting like the furniture of the planting scheme. These plants give movement, colour variation and seasonal drama. This layer is also ideal for repetition and variation to create rhythm and flow. Use ornamental grasses, ferns, lady's mantle (Alchemilla), hostas or Heuchera. These plants sway in the breeze, blur hard lines, and gently frame paths or seating zones. They offer a mix of foliage forms – arching, spiky, ruffled or mounded – which helps contrast and enrich texture.

Structural layer (80 cm–2 m+)

This layer is the backbone of your planting – the sculptural elements that create verticality and anchor the space. They provide vertical accents, shade and seasonal structure. Use small trees like Acer palmatum, Amelanchier and Cornus, or architectural shrubs like boxwood, dwarf pine or Viburnum. These offer year-round form and a sense of maturity, even in younger gardens. Also consider bamboo, tall grasses or multi-stemmed trees for a lighter architectural feel.

Tips for grouping and placement

- Group in odd numbers. Plant in threes or fives for a more organic look. Odd numbers are easier on the eye and mimic natural growth patterns.
- Repeat, don't clone. Repetition creates rhythm and calm, especially in Japandi design. But avoid using plants in strict rows or perfect grids – nature prefers gentle variation.
- Think foliage first. Flowers come and go, but leaves stay longer. Focus on texture, shape and colour of foliage to create contrast – matte versus glossy, rounded versus linear, deep green versus silver.
- Soften transitions. Let plants step gently from tall to low. Abrupt height changes can feel jarring; soft gradients between layers help the garden feel cohesive and flowing.
- Use plants to frame. Tall grasses or shrubs can act like curtains, gently screening views or framing key focal points like a sculpture, water feature or seating spot.
- Play with height. Vary heights with pot stands, low stools or built-in benches and group by mood or texture, not just plant type.

Biomorphic forms

Biomorphic forms – shapes inspired by nature, like leaves, branches or flowing water – are often found in Japandi interiors, and they translate beautifully to outdoor spaces, too. Let plant silhouettes guide your design: the arch of a fern, the fan of a maple leaf or the upright rhythm of grasses. These organic shapes soften hard lines and bring quiet movement into your garden. Use them in planting beds, curved benches or even stepping stone patterns.

Plant vessels

In Japandi design, the vessel is as significant as the plant it holds. A potted plant transforms into a living sculpture. Vessels offer flexibility in ever-changing conditions and are perfect for poor soil, limited space, or when your design calls for contrast and clarity. They're ideal for placing plants on terraces or balconies without any ground at all. With a vessel, you can tailor the soil to suit the specific needs of each plant you choose.

In traditional Japanese gardens, plant pots were used sparingly, primarily for bonsai or carefully arranged accent plants in Tsubo-niwa (see page 78). The focus was always on achieving harmony between the vessel, the plant and the surrounding space.

Scandinavian gardens, especially urban courtyards and summer cabins, rely on plant pots for flexibility. You'll often find birch saplings in wooden barrels, herbs in terracotta vessels and heather in zinc planters.

It probably won't surprise you that these vessels are made of natural materials – for example, unglazed terracotta, which is earthy and breathable, muted glazed ceramics in beige, warm grey, soft reds or moss green, raw concrete for a more minimalist and grounding vibe, or dark metal or rusted Corten steel for a more modern and bolder/stronger look.

Let the shape of the vessel echo the plant's form. A rounded vessel suits soft grasses or mounding perennials. A tall, slender vessel suits vertical growth, like bamboo or iris.

Styling vessels – calm clusters and quiet focus

In Japandi-style outdoor spaces, potted plants offer a wonderful way to add structure, softness and seasonal interest without needing full garden beds. Whether you're curating a serene balcony or enhancing the edges of a garden, vessels are versatile design tools that balance function with beauty.

In a larger outdoor space, vessels can act as movable accents:

- Framing a seating area or pathway with tall grasses or small trees like Japanese maple or dwarf pine.
- Softening architectural edges such as stairs, gravel paths or the base of walls.
- Adding vertical interest in vessels where in-ground planting isn't possible, such as on stone patios or terraces.

In a smaller outdoor space, like a small garden or a balcony:

- Create zones, like a corner 'lounge' area with a potted olive or bay tree behind a chair.
- Add privacy by using tall planters with bamboo, Miscanthus or even espaliered shrubs.
- Layer height and texture – place some vessels directly on the floor, others on low stools, crate-style risers or built-in ledges.
- Make the most of compact balconies that benefit from repetition and simplicity. Keep the colour palette tight and use plants that thrive in containers and limited sunlight.

Creating harmony when styling vessels:

- Try clustering vessels in asymmetrical groups. Use three to five vessels per grouping for a visually calming rhythm – odd numbers feel more natural.
- Use different heights and widths, but keep materials and colours harmonious.
- Combine plant forms: one upright (e.g., boxwood or tall grass), one low and mounded (e.g., lavender or heuchera) and one trailing (e.g., creeping Jenny or ivy).
- Take care with proportions: your plant should be well balanced with the vessel – neither too small nor overly large.

Take note of the microclimate, as vessels dry out faster than in-ground soil. Water regularly, and consider self-watering inserts or lining the inside with a moisture-retentive layer.

Checklist: Seasonal care

Every season brings its own tasks to keep your garden thriving. This checklist helps you stay on top of what to prune, plant, clean, and prepare - whether your space is a small balcony, courtyard, or larger garden. By following the rhythm of the year, you'll make maintenance easier and ensure your outdoor space always feels cared for and inviting.

Spring – awakening and preparation

- ☐ Refresh topsoil in pots and borders; add compost where needed.
- ☐ Prune dead or damaged branches to shape your structural plants.
- ☐ Begin feeding perennials with an organic slow-release fertilizer.
- ☐ Reposition pots if needed – rotate to balance sun exposure.
- ☐ Clean moss or gravel areas gently to allow air and light in.

Summer – growth and balance

- ☐ Water early in the day to avoid evaporation and reduce stress.
- ☐ Deadhead faded blooms to encourage more flowers and neaten appearance.
- ☐ Shade vulnerable pots in extreme heat using parasols or taller plants.
- ☐ Group potted plants for easier watering and stronger visual cohesion.
- ☐ Observe layering – adjust placement for shade/sun balance.

Autumn – transition and protection

- ☐ Cut back faded perennials but leave seed heads for winter interest.
- ☐ Begin insulating sensitive pots (wrap or move them gradually).
- ☐ Reduce watering, especially for drought-tolerant species.
- ☐ Collect fallen leaves to use as mulch or compost.
- ☐ Plant bulbs for spring – especially in pots or between ground layers.

Winter – rest and readiness

- ☐ Protect pots from freezing. Plants in pots are more vulnerable to frost than those in the ground, because their roots are exposed to cold air on all sides.
- ☐ Raise your pots off the ground with wooden blocks or pot feet to improve drainage and reduce frost damage from frozen surfaces.
- ☐ Group pots together in a sheltered spot (like close to a wall or under an eave) to create a microclimate.
- ☐ Wrap pots in jute or fleece (especially terracotta or ceramic) to prevent cracking and protect roots.
- ☐ For sensitive plants, move pots temporarily into a cold frame, garage or insulated greenhouse.
- ☐ Sweep snow off container surfaces to prevent cracking.
- ☐ Avoid watering during frosty spells to prevent root damage.
- ☐ Clean tools and empty pots for storage.

Tygo

Thank you

Firstly, I would like to thank you for reading my book and in doing so helping me do what I love. Of course, a big thanks to all the owners of the photos I have used and to the people who created the stunning places you see in my book. Special thanks to Noël van Mierlo.

Finding my ikigai sometimes was a pretty bumpy journey, so I would like to thank my friends and family for their endless support and belief in me during my journey and every day still. Special thanks to my mother Ariane, my father Leo, my brother Sander and my dear friend Marloes. I would also love to thank my boyfriend Wouter, for dealing with my chaotic brain, for supporting my good and sometimes not so good ideas, for his (not naturally given) patience, for making me laugh and for bringing calm in the storm, for being such a sweet dad to our son Tygo and making me fall in love with him all over again. And, of course, thanks to my lovely cat, the cute, fluffy and beautiful Kiyomi, for her good mood – all day, every day.

I would also love to thank Marlous. She is not only the best at what she does but I also love our talks about all kinds of things and, of course, about our cats. She has a very calming effect when I'm not seeing something clearly and am in need of support, so I'm happy that we've been able to work together on all the books. Thanks to Carolijn and Eline from Lannoo. It was my first time working with Eline but it felt like we've known each other for years. I would also like to thank Tina for her creativity and input.

I absolutely loved writing this book and taking the Japandi (life)style outdoors. Mostly I'm focused on Japandi interior design and lifestyle, like in my first two books, so personally I loved diving into outdoor spaces and learning new things myself. Being pregnant when I started writing – and becoming a mum half way through – was a bit of a challenge sometimes but also a lovely way to find a new balance for myself.

I would love to dedicate this book to our son Tygo, who was born at the beginning of this year. I hope my journey will inspire him to choose his own path, dare to make mistakes, be bold and do things he has never done before, but most importantly to do what he loves and what gives him energy. Looking forward to supporting him in the same way my family and friends support me, and allowing him to find his own ikigai.

Love, Laila

Credits

p. 4 | Van Mierlo Tuinen
Experience your Nature
www.vanmierlotuinen.nl
@vanmierlotuinen

p. 6 | Stones & Walls
Photographer: Anna Andersen

p. 8 | Photographer: Ellis Roeterdink-Mos
Dame met de lens
@damemetdelens

p. 10 | Bolia

p. 12 & 15 | Van Mierlo Tuinen
Experience your Nature
www.vanmierlotuinen.nl
@vanmierlotuinen
p. 15: Photographer: Caroline Piek

p. 16-17 | Numazu Club
Photographer: Ben Richards

p. 18 | &Tradition

p. 21 | Courtesy of GUBI

p. 22 | Top left to bottom right
- 101 Copenhagen
- Courtesy of GUBI
- Viktoria Askerow
  @tthese_beautiful_thingss
- Norm Architects - Fjord Boat House
  Photographer: Jonas Bjerre-Poulsen

p. 24-25 | Bolia

p. 27 | Refined Family Home
Design: Grand&Johnson
Styling: Rianne Landstra
Photo: Flare Department

p. 29 | Van Mierlo Tuinen
Experience your Nature
www.vanmierlotuinen.nl
@vanmierlotuinen

p. 30-31 | Numazu Club
Photographer: Ben Richards

p. 33 | Norm Architects - Forest Retreat
Photographer: Jonas Bjerre-Poulsen

p. 34, 36 &37 | Norm Architects
Sjöparken
Photographer: Jonas Bjerre-Poulsen
Interior Design by Hedda Klar

p. 39 | Numazu Club
Photographer: Ben Richards

p. 40 & 42-43 | Van Mierlo Tuinen
Experience your Nature
www.vanmierlotuinen.nl
@vanmierlotuinen
Photographer: Philippe Perdereau

p. 45 | &Tradition

p. 46-47 | Numazu Club
Photographer: Ben Richards

p. 48 | Top left to bottom right
- Courtesy of GUBI
- &Tradition
- &Tradition
- blomus

p. 51 | Viktoria Askerow
@tthese_beautiful_thingss

p. 52-53 | Bolia

p. 54 | Audo Copenhagen

p. 57 | Stones & Walls
Photographer: Anna Andersen

p. 58-59 | Cane-line

p. 61, 62-63 | Thor Alvis - Unsplash

p. 64 | Top: Arthur Tseng - Unsplash
Bottom: Bryan White - Unsplash

p. 66 & 67 | Numazu Club
Photographer: Ben Richards

p. 69 & 70-71 | Photographers:
Ariane and Leo Rietbergen

p. 72 | Top left to bottom right
- Van Mierlo Tuinen
  Experience your Nature
  www.vanmierlotuinen.nl
  @vanmierlotuinen
  Photographer: Hans Gorter
- Viktoria Askerow
  @tthese_beautiful_thingss
- Annika Zetterman
  New Nordic Gardens
- Van Mierlo Tuinen
  Experience your Nature

p. 74 | Stephane Bernard - Unsplash

p. 76 | Design: MRDK
Photographer: David Dworkind

p. 79 | Villa Verde
Photographer: Mr. Frank photography
@mr_frank_photo
Homeowner: Helga Gillé
Residents: Jorgo & Tina

p. 81 | &Tradition

p. 82-83 | Audo Copenhagen

p. 85 | &Tradition

p. 86 | Top left to bottom right
- Top two: Viktoria Askerow
  @tthese_beautiful_thingss
- Courtesy of GUBI
- Viktoria Askerow
  @tthese_beautiful_thingss

p. 88 & 89 | Viktoria Askerow
@tthese_beautiful_thingss

p. 91 | Top left to bottom right
- &Tradition
- blomus
- blomus
- &Tradition

p. 92, 93 & 94-95 | Norm Architects
Kent Avenue Penthouse
Photographer: Jonas Bjerre-Poulsen

p. 96 | Top left to bottom right
- Annika Zetterman
  New Nordic Gardens
- Van Mierlo Tuinen
  Experience your Nature
  www.vanmierlotuinen.nl
  @vanmierlotuinen
  Photographer: Hans Gorter
- Annika Zetterman
  New Nordic Gardens
- Van Mierlo Tuinen
  Experience your Nature

p. 98 | Stones & Walls
Photographer: Mirto Iatropoulou

p. 99 | &Tradition

p. 101 | Top left to bottom right
- Flare Department
  Interior design & development:
  Nadina Plomer
- Studio HENK
- Stones & Walls
  Photographer: Mirto Iatropoulou
- Flare Department
  Design & Development: Fort Staete

p. 102 & 103 | Courtesy of GUBI

p. 105 | Norm Architects
Fjord Boat House
Photographer: Jonas Bjerre-Poulsen

p. 106 | Annika Zetterman
New Nordic Gardens

p. 110-111 | Refined Family Home
Design: Grand&Johnson
Styling: Rianne Landstra
Photo: Flare Department

p. 112-135 | Van Mierlo Tuinen
Experience your Nature
www.vanmierlotuinen.nl
@vanmierlotuinen

p. 137 | Audo Copenhagen

p. 138-139 | Van Mierlo Tuinen
Experience your Nature
www.vanmierlotuinen.nl
@vanmierlotuinen

p. 140 | Flare Department
Design: Emi en Dustin Heerkens

p. 142 & 143 | Design: MRDK
Photographer: David Dworkind

p. 145 | Top left to bottom right
- Van Mierlo Tuinen
  Experience your Nature
  www.vanmierlotuinen.nl
  @vanmierlotuinen
- Van Mierlo Tuinen
  Photographer: Caroline Piek
- Van Mierlo Tuinen
  Photographer: Caroline Piek
- Van Mierlo Tuinen
  Photographer: Philippe Perdereau

p. 146-147 | Van Mierlo Tuinen
Experience your Nature
www.vanmierlotuinen.nl
@vanmierlotuinen

p. 148 | Top left to bottom right
- blomus
- Stones & Walls
  Photographer: Anna Andersen
- Stones & Walls
  Photographer: Anna Andersen
- blomus

p. 150 | Cane-line

p. 151 | Norm Architects
Kent Avenue Penthouse
Photographer: Jonas Bjerre-Poulsen

p. 153 | Stones & Walls
Photographer: Mirto Iatropoulou

p. 154 | Bolia

p. 155 | Stones & Walls
Photographer: Mirto Iatropoulou

p. 156 | Photographers:
Ariane & Leo Rietbergen

p. 158 | Design: MRDK
Photographer: David Dworkind

p. 159 | Studio HENK

p. 161 | Norm Architects
Fjord Boat House
Photographer: Jonas Bjerre-Poulsen

p. 162-163 | Konga CPH
Photographer: Dovaldė Butėnaitė
Created in collaboration with Danish architect Mette Fredskild

p. 165 | Top left to bottom right
- Studio HENK
- Grand&Johnson
  Photo: Flare Department
- &Tradition
- Refined Family Home
  Design: Grand&Johnson
  Styling: Rianne Landstra
  Photo: Flare Department

p. 166-167 | Ecohotel El Agua
@Ecohotel_El_Agua
Photographer: Nesrine Brikci
@Lescalevoyage

p. 168 | Top left to bottom right
- &Tradition
- Courtesy of GUBI
- Bolia
- Audo Copenhagen

p. 169-170 | blomus

p. 173 | Top left to bottom right
- Bolia
- Studio HENK
- Cane-line
- Bolia

p. 174 | Top left to bottom right
- Studio HENK
- Bolia
- Bolia
- Cane-line

p. 177 | Bolia

p. 178 | &Tradition

p. 179 | Audo Copenhagen

p. 180 | blomus

p. 183 | Top left to bottom right
- Cane-line
- blomus
- blomus
- Cane-line

p. 184 | Bolia

p. 185 | 101 Copenhagen

p. 186-187 | Courtesy of GUBI

p. 188 | Top left to bottom right
- Ecohotel El Agua
  @Ecohotel_El_Agua
  Photographer: Nesrine Brikci
  @Lescalevoyage
- &Tradition
- Courtesy of GUBI
- Audo Copenhagen

p. 191 | Top left to bottom right
- Cane-line
- &Tradition
- Cane-line
- Courtesy of GUBI

p. 192-193 | Courtesy of GUBI

p.194 | Stones & Walls
Photographer: Mirto Iatropoulou

p. 196-197 | Stones & Walls
Photographer: Anna Andersen

p. 199 | Top left to bottom right
- blomus
- Cane-line
- Audo Copenhagen
- Cane-line

p. 200 & 201 | Design: MRDK
Photographer: David Dworkind

p. 202 | Top left to bottom right
- Audo Copenhagen
- Audo Copenhagen
- Cane-line
- &Tradition

p. 204 | &Tradition

p. 205 | Courtesy of GUBI

p. 207 & 209 | Norm Architects
Forest Retreat
Photographer: Jonas Bjerre-Poulsen

p. 210-211 | Design: MRDK
Photographer: David Dworkind

p. 212, 215, 216-217, 218, 221, 222-223 & 225 | Van Mierlo Tuinen
Experience your Nature
www.vanmierlotuinen.nl
@vanmierlotuinen
p. 216-217: Photographer:
Robert Koelewijn

p. 226 | Annika Zetterman
New Nordic Gardens

p. 229 | Van Mierlo Tuinen
Experience your Nature
www.vanmierlotuinen.nl
@vanmierlotuinen

p. 230 | Viktoria Askerow
@tthese_beautiful_thingss

p. 233, 234-235, 236 & 239 |
Van Mierlo Tuinen
Experience your Nature
www.vanmierlotuinen.nl
@vanmierlotuinen

p. 240 | Top left to bottom right
- Cane-line
- Audo Copenhagen
- Audo Copenhagen
- Cane-line

p. 243 | 101 Copenhagen

p. 244 | Top left to bottom right
- 101 Copenhagen
- Audo Copenhagen
- Viktoria Askerow
  @tthese_beautiful_thingss
- 101 Copenhagen

p. 245 & 246 | Viktoria Askerow
@tthese_beautiful_thingss

p. 247 | Top left to bottom right
- Top left: Cane-line
- Other three: Audo Copenhagen

p. 250-251 | My own garden
Residents: Laila, Wouter, Tygo & Kiyomi

p. 252 | My lovely cat Kiyomi
Photographer: Ellis Roeterdink-Mos
Dame met de lens
@damemetdelens

Colophon

Concept and text: Laila Rietbergen, @japandi.interior
Text: Marlous Snijder
Editing: Heather Sills
Book design: Tina De Souter Bookdesign

THEMA: AMV, WJK, AMCR
D/2025/45/555
ISBN: 978-90-209-7328-0

www.lannoo.com

Sign up for our newsletter with news about new and forthcoming publications on art, interior design, food and travel, photography and fashion as well as exclusive offers and events. If you have any questions or comments about the material in this book, please do not hesitate to contact our editorial team: art@lannoo.com

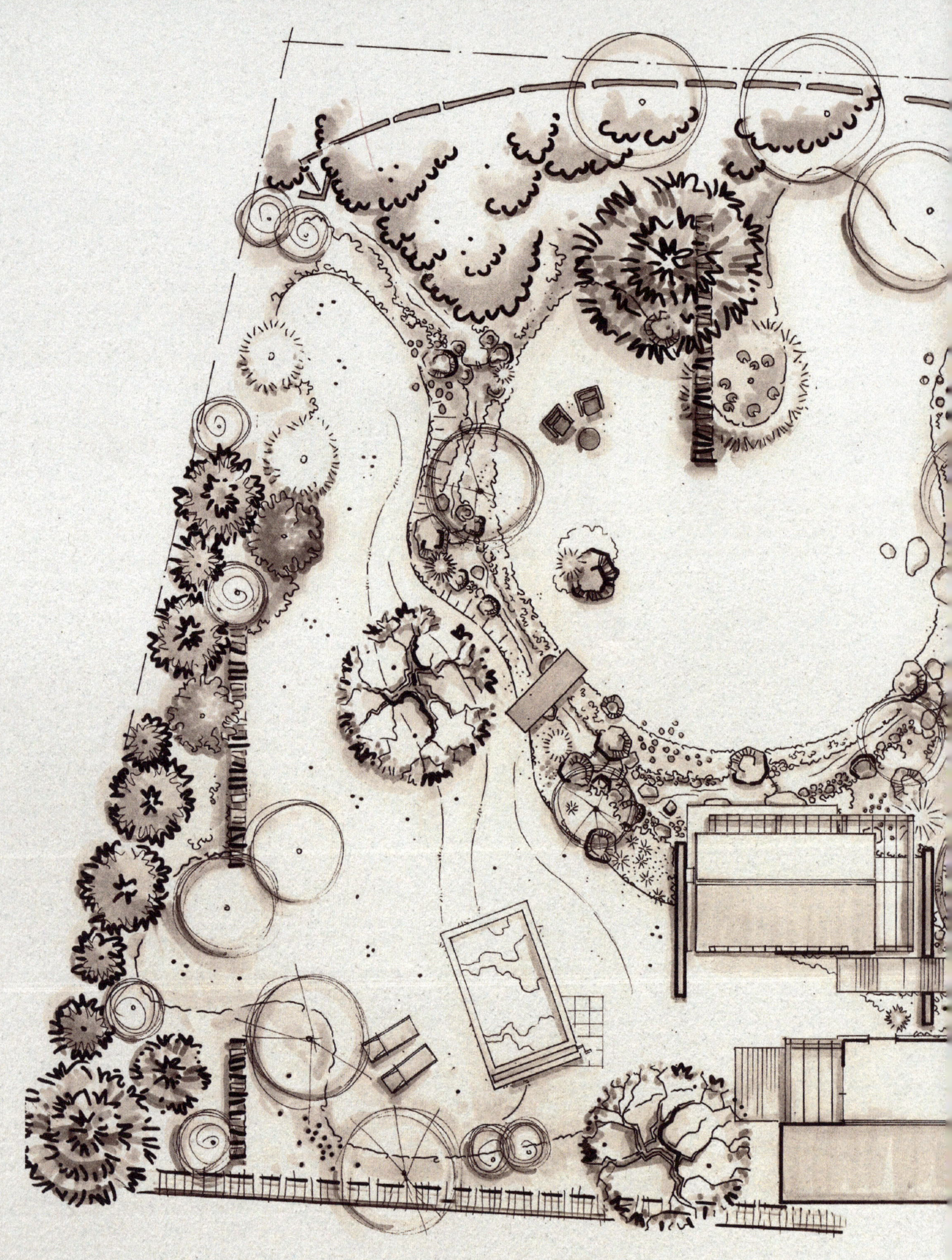